tales from a

Tuscan
Table

ISBN 13: 978-0-9794503-0-3
ISBN 10: 0-9794503-0-6

Design & Layout by
JPDesigns
greatdesignforless@mindspring.com

Brandon's Printing
6725 Jimmy Carter Blvd.
Norcross, GA 30071

tales from a
Tuscan
Table

10 years of cooking class misadventures
and culinary mayhem
in glorious Tuscany

With Recipes from the Region

by Chef John Wilson

The Names Have Been Changed To Protect The Guilty!

I would like to dedicate this book to my mother

Adelaide Frances Emanuel Wilson

For she instilled in me an appreciation for great food.

And to my father, the late

John H. Wilson

Who was always ready for an adventure in good eating.

contents

uno

And They Called *Me* High Maintenance

ABOUT TEN YEARS AGO, I left the restaurant business to try and find something new and different. After a quarter century of ceaseless toil in the food industry, I'd lost touch with what I loved about cooking in the first place. I needed to find another avenue, one in which I could once again be creative and challenge myself — and make a living doing it. Since I'm not afraid of work, I was willing to consider just about anything that would draw on my skills as a restaurant chef and caterer.

Preferably it would be something I could do alone, or with a minimal crew to assist me. I'd had my fill of managing people. In the restaurant business, a manager inevitably becomes a father figure to his staff, and finds himself spending much of his time motivating them, inspiring them... sometimes just encouraging to get them to come to work every day. What I wanted now was to do my job — to work hands-on in the kitchen — while hiring others to do whatever else was necessary; for example, keeping the books.

All the same, I understood that you can't run a business without doing some managing along the way; you have to instill others with your vision, with a love of quality, with what you require of them for a job well done. Once this groundwork has been laid, ideally your enterprise will run like a well-tuned engine.

The more I considered all this, the more difficult it seemed to achieve. I'd been in restaurants so long, it was hard even to think outside that reality. But it was a reality I was determined to put behind me. I'd given it everything I could, and it was time to move on.

I'd just quit my last full-time restaurant job, as Food and Beverage Director of Fernbank Museum of Natural History in Atlanta. During my first week, I worked 79 hours; and it didn't get much better over the succeeding three years.

When I came on board, I changed the entire operation, never asking for permission, only forgiveness when I needed to. I established a catering department; persuaded upper management to purchase a liquor license; and in diverse other ways created for myself a monster far outside my original job description.

As the food and beverage director of a nonprofit institution, you can wear many hats in the course of your daily rounds. And since I'm a driven, Type-A kind of guy, I wore them all. I prepared the foods, hired the staff, did management training and food costing, ordered all foods and liquor for both the café and the catering division — and so on, seemingly endlessly.

And somewhere along the way... I lost the magic. So after three years (which, given the hours I'd worked, was the equivalent of six) I said goodbye, and thus found myself wondering "What next?"

The quest took me to France, where I knew I could collect my thoughts, soak in some inspiration, and witness a better quality of life firsthand. And France, God bless her... France didn't fail me.

When I got back home, I started my business, Culinary Vacations. The idea was simple: I would return again to France — and to other great culinary capitals of Europe — and this time I'd take people with me. These students would spend a week learning to cook regional favorites based on seasonal ingredients, and they'd soak in the local color and culture as well. I'd share my love of cooking with others in an endeavor that would involve all of my creative faculties, and I'd get to do it in the places I loved best. And maybe I could make a living at it!

It's worked out beautifully, and I exult in the freedom and fun. I still wear many hats; I create all the recipes for each class and personally print them, bind them, and bring them with me to Europe; I serve as host and master-of-ceremonies for my students during their time with me; I supervise them in the kitchen, instructing them in the lore of the region and the techniques and tricks of preparing each dish, the wonderful alchemy of turning a batch of ingredients into an irresistible meal.

I also do all the grocery shopping, tote the luggage, serve as chauffeur, and wash the van each Sunday before I pick up my eager students. Teach the daily cooking classes, open the wine, and drive the van to all of the excursions. Wash the kitchen towels, make a fire in the fireplace when needed and cook the other two meals of the day. I make the beds on the weekends, clear the dishes after the meals, and even mop the floor if needed. Act as tour guide and assistance when needed for the overseas phone calls and gift suggestions for loved ones back home. Not to mention wine buyer and part time dish washer. Sometimes it seems as though I'm still working eighty-hour weeks; many of these chores could easily be handed over to an employee, leaving me free to focus on the tasks that need my special skills. But when you start a business, there isn't the money for an employee; and then, once you're established, it's hard to delegate the tasks to someone else. After all, you've been doing them for so long, and you know how to do them best.

So I'm surprised when a student in Tuscany suddenly calls me "high maintenance." It's at the very beginning of the week — right after I've provided everyone with a printed apron and given instructions to care for them . "They're your responsibility now," I say.

"Wow, you're really high maintenance," this student shoots back as she fastens the apron around her waist. It's a startling thing to hear from someone who hasn't even got to know me and understand the way I do things. For a moment I wonder whether she really knows what "high maintenance" means; but of course she does. She must, because her husband Henry is of that persuasion.

I know the type well: white-collar executives who require an entourage to run and fetch for them all day, every day. It's a shock for such people to find themselves at Culinary Vacations. Here, each of us does his or her own cooking — even to the washing of the vegetables. So it's a bit of surprise for a self-proclaimed Master Of the Universe to suddenly have to find the grater in the cabinet on his own. But I insist on it; it is a cooking *school*, after all.

And cook we do. We chop and dice and sometimes get a little dirty.

The work is not, however, exceedingly difficult, and the only stress is self-inflicted. I try not to be too demanding of anyone's cooking abilities during the week; often different students are at different levels of expertise, so I strive to tailor my recommendations and suggestions to each person's needs. My goal is to help you become a better cook, to make things easier for you when you return home and start preparing meals on your own.

I've had several genuinely "high maintenance" types descend on my school, and it never fails to astonish me that they'll pay for the trip and classes, then arrive and express shock that they have to prepare their own meals — and from the basic ingredients, too. They really can't believe they're expected to strap on an apron every day and chop, dice, sear, and sauté.

Take Henry, for instance. Each day he seems completely at sea, battering me with an unending litany of questions:

"Hey, Chef John, where do I find the peeler?"

"So which cabinet is the sugar hiding in?"

"Excuse me, how do you work this scale to get a tare weight?"

...and so on, and so on. It would actually be less work for me if, instead of answering all his questions, I just made his dish for him.

And the irony is, I've already answered all his questions, and in exhaustive detail. On Sunday evening, when everyone's arrived, I gather them in the kitchen and go over the location of all the ingredients. I demonstrate how to operate the oven, stovetop, and kitchen scale. I explain which herbs are growing in the garden, and in which cabinets you'll find the skillets, pasta pots, and linens.

Most people take all this in, and the week goes smoothly. But not the high-maintenance Henrys, who apparently think my detailed speech is some kind of performance art, or just me satisfying a craving for attention.

Each day at Culinary Vacations, a student is assigned a recipe, either to complete on his own or with another student. When I have two Henrys in one week, I like to team them up, then stand back and watch what happens. Sometimes they work together beautifully and get the recipe done. Other times they end up like two dogs in an alley, snarling over turf. I usually play it safe by giving them an easy recipe; if I don't, I'm just asking for more work for myself.

Henry and I eventually make it through the week, though without forging any special bond. Which is fine for both of us; we'll never see each other again. Although... sometimes I'm surprised. Against all odds, the most high-maintenance students will get home and realize that they've actually learned something. A seed has been planted, a curiosity born. And, amazingly, they'll come back to me for another vacation, with greater humility and a genuine curiosity to learn.

This would be a very big surprise with Henry, however.

On Friday, after a lunch cooking class, I load up the students in the van to take them back to the train station in Florence — all but Henry and his wife, who have arranged for a driver to come fetch them and take them to the Amalfi Coast and beyond.

As I'm staggering out the door, weighed down by luggage and calling out orders to organize the departure — the usual rushing around to handle the last-minute details — Henry comes out to ask for tissue.

"The box in our room is empty," he says.

I glance at my watch. "Henry, I'm leaving in two minutes. Your car isn't coming for another two hours."

"I know," he says, with a hint of impatience in his voice. "That's why I need the tissue from you *now*." He laughs a little, as if in exasperation at how thick I am.

"You can't spend two hours without tissue?" I ask, and he looks at me as though I've just suggested something faintly obscene.

"*Our box is empty,*" he repeats more insistently — as though this trumps any argument I might give him. Behind me, students are clambering into the van, shoving luggage in where luggage isn't meant to go. I have to get back to them.

"Henry," I say, "I'm so sorry there isn't any more tissue. I only stocked up for one week. The week is over." And I'm thinking to myself, *For God's sake, you can see I'm in a hurry here; use a bit of toilet tissue. Just this once!*

High Maintenance

And it's not just men who are afflicted. Oh, no. High maintenance individuals come in both genders. Take a certain mother and daughter whom I find accompanying me to Provence. Now, I've had several such pairings over the years. Sometimes a woman will bring her daughter to atone for never having taught her any kitchen skills when she was growing up.

Other times, it's just a nice way to travel together, reconnect, and share experiences, especially if both women like to cook.

This particular mother and daughter, however — Connie and Trish — are of a different kind altogether. I get the impression the trip was Trish's idea, and that she's invited her mother out of pity or duty. Certainly the woman is utterly dependent on her. She calls out to her nonstop during the cooking lessons:

"Trish, where'd you get that garlic?"

"Trish, what do you call this herb again?"

"Trish, where do I find that mezzaluna?"

"Trish...Trish...Trish...Trish..."

I begin to wince whenever I hear the name.

And the kicker is, Connie and Trish aren't even a team. I've given each woman a separate recipe, in an attempt to force Connie to stand on her own two feet. But she never even tries; at every step, she calls her daughter away from her own work to help her.

Now, before each class begins, I pull most of the ingredients I know each recipe requires, in order to make it easier for everyone to find them. That's why I go over the location of all ingredients and utensils on the first day. It would be so much easier on the group if everyone just *paid attention*. But obviously some people feel they don't have to. Why bother, when they've got a Trish to do it for them?

So you can see why I might be taken aback at being called "high maintenance" — just because I'd set a few rules and suggested students look after their own aprons. In fact I do everything I can to make things as smooth and stress-free as possible for my students. I'm not so much *high maintenance* as *my maintenance*. I'm the one with the mop in his hands at the end of the day. In most cases I wouldn't even know how to let someone do the work for me. But someday when I win the lottery, I'll gladly pass the bucket and soap to the next guy and give high living a whirl.

At the end of the week, Trish tells me what a great time she's had, how much she's learned, how she's loved seeing a European country and enjoyed the excursions I planned for them. She's so enthusiastic she wants to come back, this time to my school in Barcelona.

"Wonderful," I say, adding after a brief pause, "and... Connie as well?"

She laughs. "Well, if you can handle it," she says, giving me a sympathetic look. "I know my mother can be a tad bit high maintenance."

Lovely lady, Trish. Welcome back anytime. As for Connie... I'll think it over.

2
due

Things You Need To Know To Blend In

MOST OF THE TIME, it's good to be an American in Europe. We like to spend money, and Europeans like us spending it where they live. Believe me, I've heard it from many a shopkeeper: they're fond of the American dollar.

But despite the welcome our Am Ex cards affords us, some of us feel a desire to go a step further, to experience Europe as the Europeans do; to become, during our stay, a little less American and a little more native. I'm that way myself. I like to get a handle on a country, its customs, culture and traditions, its way of doing things.

I don't look Italian by any stretch of the imagination. At 6´2˝, I literally stick out among crowds of continentals, and though I'm somewhat slender as Europeans tend to be, during certain times of the year I inevitably put on a few extra pounds. So it isn't easy for me to blend in, but I try. For instance, I always learn and practice a few words in the language of my host country. Using simple greetings and small phrases may not fool the locals into thinking you're one of them, but it does show them you respect their culture and are making an effort to appreciate it.

And of course having some familiarity with the language comes in especially handy in restaurants. You can successfully avoid contact with the locals, until you find yourself in a restaurant; then you're forced to converse with the server to get your food. Now, all Europeans have had six years of English in school, and most are still able to speak it. But if your server for some reason can't — or even if he can —it's a chance to practice your language skills. One more opportunity to blend in a little.

Once you've ordered, there are other customs you can follow, certain Italian practices that are different from the way we Americans dine. I like to know from my Italian friends just what is protocol and what isn't; what's considered proper and what's a breach of etiquette. Because I teach in Italy, these are valuable things to pass on to my students.

For instance, in Italy, there's no rush at the table; no one hurries through dinner. While American eat to live, Europeans live to eat. And yet despite the hours they spend over their meals, Europeans are as a rule quite slim; Americans far outweigh the rest of the world — though some countries are starting to catch up (largely because they've adopted our frantic, erratic eating habits and demanding schedules).

Americans can get very uneasy when dining for three hours. We have things to do, places to go, monuments to see. But when you sit down at an Italian restaurant, the manager presumes you will be the only diners at that table that evening. Unless you're in a high tourist area. There, the tables may be used more than once per night. (But you should try to avoid dining in high tourist areas anyway.) So when you make a reservation and you arrive early?... No problem, your table is waiting for you. Likewise, arriving late is not a worry — though too late, and your table may have been given away. As an American, I like to dine early and go to bed early, so I make my reservation as soon as the restaurant opens. I get better service and my evening doesn't stretch into the wee hours.

I've learned to relax at an Italian table and enjoy the long meal. It's one of the pleasures of working in Europe six months of the year. But I wouldn't even think of having dinner with my mother there; she wants to get in and get out. She's got places to go!... I'm not sure where, but darn it, she's itchy to get there. So a three-hour dinner is out of the question for her; she'd jump out of her skin. Most of us, however, can learn to slow down, savor the moment, the wonderful food, and enjoy conversing with the person across the table. Even if you're on your own, you can enjoy the slower pace. I dine alone frequently in Europe, so I always bring a book with me. I get quite a lot of reading done, which is wonderful. I find it an ideal time to get lost in a story.

Beyond these general principles, there are a few specific guidelines I can give you for blending in while in Tuscany, most of which come by way of former students, or indeed I myself, having first broken the rules and thus learned the hard way.

Don't use olive oil as a dip for your bread.

I'm invited to dinner at the home of my Italian neighbor, an artist named Albarosa. (If you've traveled with me in Tuscany, you'll know whom I'm talking about.) On her table is a basket of sliced bread. In Italy, at almost every table — whether in a restaurant or someone's home — you'll always find olive oil and vinegar along with salt and pepper. Italians dash oil onto just about everything: soup, vegetables, fruits, you name it. It's the famous Mediterranean Diet.

I like olive oil for my bread, especially in Tuscany because the breads there are so bland. There's no salt added; it's just their way of baking it. So as I'm watching Albarosa cook, I take a slice of bread, pour a little olive oil onto my plate and dip the bread into it, then savor the wonderfully warm, golden taste.

Albarosa turns and sees me, and almost drops her wooden spoon. "What on earth are you doing?" she asks in a decidedly curt tone, as though she's caught me rubbing food onto the countertops, or eating with my feet.

I'm taken aback by her shock. "It's what we do in the States," I say. This doesn't seem to appease her — after all, what don't we do in the States? — so I continue "All the Italian restaurants provide little dishes of oil for your bread. Sometimes they even grate Parmesan cheese into it, or cracked black pepper, or even Balsamic vinegar." Her look of horror increases, and I add sheepishly, "They say it's Italian."

"Well, it's not!" she vehemently assures me. "Don't ever do that in public, especially when you're with me. In fact, just don't do it at all!" She emphatically repeats that it is not an Italian habit, but by now I've gotten the message loud and clear.

Thanks to Albarosa, whenever I visit an Italian-American restaurant and the server makes a great show of ceremoniously pouring the very green extra-virgin olive oil onto a plate and then proceeds to top it with fresh-ground pepper and mix in a smidgen of grated Parmesan, all the while telling me, "This is the way Italians take their bread" — I shoot back, "In what part of Italy do they do it this way?" Or, "When was the last time you had bread served to you this way in Italy?" The only answer I ever receive is the deer-in-the-headlights look you might expect.

Don't ask for butter for your bread.

It's the day before a Culinary Vacations week officially begins, and a family has arrived early. I don't encourage this, as I've discovered I need my space before plunging into the work week. But this time I allow it with the proviso that my guests pay me a small stipend for the extra nights lodging, and also treat me to dinner.

It's not often I get an entire family group; and indeed in this case, the father — George — isn't staying for the class. He's just accompanied his wife Rachel, and daughter Mary, after a holiday in Florence together, and will be leaving them tomorrow and returning home.

Even though they've already been in Italy several days, I gather them together before we go out and explain some of the do's and don't's of Italian restaurants, thinking that they'll appreciate some pointers on how to blend in — or at least how not to stand out so much.

As it happens, they couldn't really care less. Rachel at least pretends to pay attention to me, but George glances constantly at his watch and Mary plays with the hem of her jacket. I think I even hear her humming. Well, some people are like that. In their view, what's the point of blending in with the natives? They'll never see these people again. They go through life that way — bold in appearance and in actions.

We end up at a local restaurant where I know the chef, his daughter, and some of their friends. It's not too far from our villa, and it's known for its wonderful Tuscan specialties. It's a popular dining spot among the locals, and doesn't seem to attract many tourists despite being located on a very busy street. It also has a superb area for dining *al fresco* when the weather permits (as it often does in Tuscany).

I've only dined here a few times before, and have longed to return. I've also wanted to bring some Americans who would respect the atmosphere of the place. It seemed I've missed the mark with this family.

We're seated square in the center of the dining room — not ideal placement, I'm thinking. I'd have preferred a corner away from the locals, so that they couldn't stare and talk about us all night. But there are no other tables available. Okay, then. Brazen it out.

While we're studying our menus, a basket of Tuscan bread arrives at the table. Rachel asks our server, who speaks no English, for butter to go with the bread. Of course he doesn't understand. But before she can clarify, I explain to her that here, buttering bread is just not done. Possibly in the north, where dairy is part of the economy, but definitely not in Tuscany.

"Well, that's plain silly," she says. "It's bread and butter." As if that closes the argument.

The waiter is still hovering, confused; I explain to him in Italian — butter, please, maggiordomo; not for me, for the lady.

He darts away and returns moments later with a few tiny scoops of butter in a small dish covered with tiny ice cubes. Now, we Americans love our butter soft and spreadable, so that it melts easily into our toast, baked potatoes, and so on. So looking at these invulnerable little yellow balls, Rachel wails, "What am I supposed to do with these?" She tries to cut into one of them and it jumps out from beneath her knife and sails off the table — nearly striking a nearby diner in the arm.

In the end, she has to wait for the butter to soften. But her troubles with the restaurant aren't over. Which brings me to rule number three.

Don't ask for ice in your water.

The waiter returns to serve our water — which is handled differently than it is at home. In the States, your glass is just automatically filled from a pitcher of tap water, free of charge. In Italy, you're asked to make a choice: acqua frizzante or acqua naturale — sparkling or still. Whichever you choose comes to you in a bottle, which you pay for. I usually tell the server I'd like a carafe of tap water. The restaurant prefers that you not request water this way because it doesn't boost the size of the bill. Also, your server doesn't like it either because his tip is based on a percentage of the bill, so if the bill's lower, so is his take. (In all of Europe, the sales tax or VAT tax and gratuity are added to the check, automatically.) Even so, I order tap water; it makes me look like a local. I'm blending in.

Rachel, however, has ordered a bottle of still water, and the waiter dutifully produces it and places it on the table before her. She picks it up to pour, but immediately puts it down again, looking frustrated.

"What's the matter?" I ask.

"It's room temperature," she says, clearly exasperated. The butter's too cold, the water's too warm... Rachel's not having a good day.

She calls the waiter back to ask for ice. Again, he doesn't understand her.

"*Ice, ice,*" she says, more loudly, as though that will help.

The waiter of course remains mystified, so I translate. *Ghiaccio per la donna.* Ice for the lady. I see him glance at the butter, which is still covered in ice, and for a moment I think he's going to take some of those cubes and just plunk them into her glass. Certainly that's what I would have done.

But no, he scurries off, then returns moments later with a very small bowl containing exactly three smallish ice cubes.

Rachel looks at it. "Is he kidding?" she says. "Those'll melt before I get them in the glass!"

"Europeans use very little ice in their drinks," I explain to her. "And usually just in cocktails."

"I'm going to *need* a cocktail after all this," she quips.

I can understand her dismay, if I try. I'm an American, too; and when I want ice, I want a lot of it. But... *never in Europe.*

Rachel's troubles only worsen as the evening rolls on, bringing us to our next rule...

Be careful about ordering red meat.

It's now time to order our meal. As a rule, Italian restaurants don't offer daily specials, so I give my recommendations to the table. I suggest not ordering meat of any kind, because you can't be entirely certain of what you're ordering.

In Europe, organ meats are regularly consumed, and that might be what you find staring at you from your plate, which isn't quite to everyone's taste. Also cuts of beef in Italy aren't the same cuts as we have in the States; so when you find a steak with a name you think you recognize, it could very well be a different piece of meat entirely.

"So my advice," I conclude, "is to avoid the beef; unless you know what you're doing, you can end up with something very fatty and filled with gristle." But Rachel is a very determined woman, used to having her own way. And she won't have it that what I'm saying is true.

"I've read so much about beefsteak *Fiorentina*," she says. "All the guidebooks recommend it when you're traveling in Tuscany." Her mind is made up. She orders the fabled steak.

The rest of the party orders a variety of dishes but wisely steers clear of red meat. Someone, at least, is finally listening to me. George appears to be the kind of man who's used to taking orders (as many husbands are). And Mary, now that she's in a crowd of Italians, suddenly seems to care more about blending in. Possibly this is due to the attention she's receiving from some handsome young Italians at other tables. She's a true blonde and Italians love blondes, which are very rare in Italy. Historically they've had to import them. It's increasingly clear that some of these dark-haired, olive-skinned Italian men would like to import Mary somewhere private after dinner.

Before Rachel's steak is grilled, the chef brings it into the dining room to show her. He nods to me, as we've met several times, then proudly presents the beautiful T-bone; it's about two-and-a-half inches thick with a nice marbling of fat on the inside, which means it will be full of flavor. *"Molto bello,"* I tell him, smiling.

Rachel, however, is visibly appalled at having the raw, red steak shoved in front of her on a platter, still quivering a bit as though not a hundred per cent dead yet. She can barely bring herself to speak.

Before long Rachel's steak returns to the table, grilled to perfection and trailing a delicious aroma. Its color is rich and gorgeous, with perfect cross-hatching across its length. Rachel shifts expectantly in her seat, flicks her tongue across her lips in anticipation, and cuts into it. We watch her take the first bite.

She chews a bit.

Then she chews a bit more.

Then she stops chewing.

I'm holding my breath.

"It's full of gristle," she says, the wad of steak still lodged inside her cheek.

There's no way she'll be able to get it down her throat, so she spits it back onto her plate. Mary is suddenly mortified that her gentlemen admirers are watching this. Rachel tries a few more bites, with no greater success.

Rachel looks up at me, her eyes bleak with defeat.

"Try some pasta," I tell her.

Never order cappuccino after 11:00 AM. (And don't expect free refills.)

Finally, we finish our meal and we'd all like coffee. Rachel specifically desires her favorite, cappuccino. I take a deep breath; I don't relish having yet one more blow to deliver to her, but I must.

"Actually," I tell her, "in Italy, they don't make cappuccino after about ten in the morning. Sometimes they'll stretch it out to eleven, but it's a morning drink, not an evening one." Rachel's beginning to look a little angry now, as though I'm making up these rules on the spot just to annoy her. "Espresso is the preferred after-dinner coffee," I tell her, and I make a little yummy noise as though this might convince her to change her mind.

But Rachel is a determined lady. And Rachel wants cappuccino.

At this point, I'm almost feeling sorry for her, so I decide that maybe she should get something she wants — just this one thing. It's far too late to blend in, we've already become a kind of spectacle to the other diners. Most of Mary's ardent admirers have given up on her, so I say "We'll ask nicely, and maybe they'll agree. But possibly they won't want to start up the steamer again after they've already cleaned it for the day."

In the end, by means of pleading and politeness and a few well-chosen Italian phrases, I persuade the waiter to make four cappuccinos, one for each of us. I reason that the kitchen staff won't be quite so upset about having to re-wash the machine if it's used to make four cups, as opposed to just one. Everyone's happy; even me.

The foamy brew arrives and somewhat restores Rachel's spirits. Happily, she puts down the empty cup and says, "I'll have another one."

I give her The Look, and she says, "What now?"

"Well," I say as gently as possible, "you realize another cup is another charge."

Her jaw drops. "But, in the States you get as many refills as you want!"

She must be getting them somewhere different from me; my Starbucks doesn't do this. But I leave that unsaid. Instead, I tell her, "Let's make the next batch at the villa" and fortunately she agrees, so we can get the bill and go. Which brings us to the next rule...

Don't add an additional amount to your receipt once it's been charged to your credit card.

In European countries you have to ask for your bill. Your server waits for you to make the request — in Italy, by calling for *il conto* — which is his indication that you're finished. It's the opposite to the way things are handled in the States, where the restaurant is eager to move you out so the next party can have your table, and your waiter therefore hovers over you as you conclude your meal, eager to slap you with the bill.

What's more, once you do request the bill, it takes a good while to arrive. Italians don't mind this, because they enjoy lingering at the table over coffee or grappa, chatting and having a fine, relaxed time. But we Americans can start to wonder if we've been forgotten. I usually ask for *il conto* when my coffee arrives. That gives them plenty of time to add up the damages while I'm still enjoying myself.

Tonight, the bill arrives and as agreed earlier, it's George's treat. He puts his charge card on the table and the waiter, seeing this, comes back with a portable charge-card machine. It's wireless! He processes the total, then hands the receipt to George — who adds on an extra amount, then signs it and hands it back.

The waiter looks a little upset and begins blurting something, and George is quite taken aback. "What's the matter?" he asks. "Didn't I leave enough?" At this point, I have to wonder how he and his family have managed to get by in Italy up to now. Possibly they've only eaten in chain restaurants that are used to Americans who demand ice and butter and cappuccinos after sundown.

Carefully I explain that in Europe, the bill is charged for the exact amount and that this is the amount that's already gone digitally sailing off to the processing facility in outer space. It's too late to change it. If you want to leave a tip beyond what's already been factored into the bill, you have to do it in cash — which I demonstrate by leaving some myself.

George shakes his head. "Crazy country," he says — echoing the other diners around him, some of whom are doubtless shaking their heads and murmuring "Crazy Americans."

A 10% charge for service is included in your bill, as well as a 20% sales tax. So when the fixed-price lunch you see advertised on a sign outside a restaurant seems a little high, remember it does include tax and gratuity. Sometimes I calculate back to determine the real price of whatever I'm ordering; then it doesn't seem quite so high.

It's just a different way of life than we're accustomed to. In some restaurants there's a fee per person that includes the linens, glass usage, salt and pepper, and so on, which it lists as a separate fee on the bill. Some restaurants will also state whether it's an additional charge or if it's included. If you're ever in doubt, you can always ask (another reason to have a few Italian phrases mastered beforehand).

I don't guarantee that if you follow my rules you'll blend in when you visit Tuscany. You will, however, avoid some easy mistakes that make you awkwardly stand out. Beyond that, blending in is more a matter of adjusting your internal clock so that you slow down, relax, and enjoy the more leisurely pace of life in the Italian heartland. It's worth the effort... you'll enjoy your time more, understand the Italian perspective better, and possibly even make some Tuscan friends. And when they come visit you in the States, you can introduce them to the wonder of free coffee refills.

tre

Kick Me

SHORTLY AFTER I GET CULINARY VACATIONS UP AND RUNNING, eight ladies organize their own group to go to Tuscany with me. I've met most of them before in Atlanta, either socially or in a business setting. As a matter of fact, most of them are former catering clients of mine, or friends of clients. They seem like a lot of fun to be with individually, so I'm confident we'll have a great time as a group. The two I haven't met, a mother and daughter, are from out of state. But really, how bad can they be... ?

The six women I've already met travel together to Venice the week before joining up with me. During that time, one of the out-of-town women — Vanessa, the mother — arrives in Florence. She calls and wants to "do lunch" with me. Frankly I'm too busy for a forty-minute drive to Florence, a meal of God knows what duration, then another forty-minute drive back... especially to be with someone I'll be basically living with in a few days' time. So I decline the invitation. Not having lunch with Vanessa is, it turns out, a bad choice on my part, a wrong business move, which I think is the reason she treats me the way she does when she finally arrives at the villa. But I'm getting ahead of myself...

Vanessa's daughter, Stacey, is the last student to arrive in Italy, the night before my classes begin. So the group has a night together in Florence to bond. The next afternoon I show up in the van and escort them all to the villa in Greve-in-Chianti.

As I expected, the women are a lot of fun on the drive, merrily re-counting their adventures and misadventures in and around Venice. Hearing other people's travel stories is a real treat for me; however, I prefer the person relating the anecdote to be a good storyteller. Not, in other words, the kind who's incapacitated by laughter throughout the tale, so that you can't follow the thread, much less understand what on earth is so blasted funny. However, I try to remain polite and smile no matter who's doing the talking. Some of the other women are less patient with each other — issuing orders to "get to the point" or just plain taking over the story from the one who started it — and observing this helps me figure out the power players in the group, the ringleaders, the ones who can make decisions the others will follow. Vanessa appears to be one of these.

When we get to the villa, things start to go downhill fast. My au-thority isn't exactly challenged, but it never seems to be acknowl-edged either. I'm viewed more as a lackey or servant than as a chef or teacher. Several times during the week, I think I must have a sign reading *Kick Me* hanging on my back, because some of the women are treating me like dirt. I can't figure out why. I'm sufficiently famil-iar with Southern women to know that if I confronted them about it, they'd sweetly apologize, say they never realized they were treat-ing me this way, that everything's wonderful and "You're an angel" — then go on behaving exactly the way they've been doing all along.

This is frustrating because I've just started this business and I'd truly appreciate genuinely constructive criticism. But I can't get any help or guidance from passive-aggressive attitudes, or from sulking and snickering. And it goes against my grain to be treated so disdain-fully by the ringleaders. Several times during the week, when some-one kindly gets up to help me clear the dishes from the table, Vanessa will say, "Oh, sit down and let John do that, it's what he's here for." Well, no; I'm here to teach cooking skills, and to introduce you to a great culinary culture.

Now, I'm not afraid of work; far from it. It's one of the reasons I formed this company — so I can run it solo, doing things the way I think they should be done. And I don't mind these little menial tasks; they're my duty as the group's *host*. But host is different from *ser-vant*; and it astonishes me when my students can't even be bothered to bring their coffee cups into the kitchen after I've cleared away the breakfast dishes. I treat them with sufficient respect to leave them enjoying their wine when I retire for the night; but they don't sufficiently respect me to do other than leave their filmy glasses strewn about the room for me to collect and wash the next morning. I am getting used to the work load.

I should add that most of my students are quite courteous; and others who aren't, are simply forgetful or sloppy. Nothing disrespectful in it. But there's something different about this group's disregard for common courtesies. It's like they're *putting me in my place.*

Still, there's no major problem I can point to — no real violation of my trust or my property. Just these little nicks and jabs. I even feel confident enough with the women to introduce them to Albarosa, my artist friend who lives across the street. The women take a liking to her and some even buy some of the works she has for sale in her studio.

Before I know it, the week is almost up. On Thursdays I always schedule an outing devoted to what I call "Village Exploration." It's a day of traveling around the countryside, seeing small villages you wouldn't normally visit on a tour bus. (Indeed, tour buses wouldn't even fit through the gates of most of them.) They really are quaint, picturesque places to admire and explore, and which give you a feeling of how rural Italians live.

Although I'm proud to show students these historic places of interest, for many of them it's really an excuse for a day of shopping. Particularly when the group is predominately female. There is no question in my mind that, *Ladies Like To Shop.*

So when we're in Castellina, one of the smaller villages on our jaunt, I show the group some small ceramic figurines, handmade locally and quite famous in the region, called *pupi.* They're only about two to five inches, and always depict people, some animals, but never inanimate objects. They're awfully darn cute; their heads, arms, and legs all move to the pull of a string. Each joint or segment is made individually, hand painted, and then joined together with twine. I'd never seen them before I found them here in Castellina. Not cheap, but unique. I have my chef *pupo* hanging in my kitchen window, and people often comment on it, many confessing that they own *pupi* as well.

We walk by a kind of hardware store with hundreds are *pupi* in its window. There are doctors, nurses, baseball and tennis players, golfers, kings and queens, elves, pirates, dancers, clowns, devils, preachers, nuns, priests, warlocks, witches, wizards — you name it. All my ladies want either the chef or the tennis player, and there are only a few of each to be had. Within a few frenzied minutes, they're all taken.

One woman, Frieda, has managed to seize the bulk of the desired pupi. Too late, she realizes that this has not made her popular with the other women who are grumbling about her grabbiness. She corners me and says, "Take us to Siena please, Chef. We can get more *pupi* there and we can all have the ones we want."

I can't believe what I'm hearing. "Frieda, do you have any idea how large Siena is? Do you even know for sure that you can buy *pupi* there?"

"You can! The shop owner here just told me so."

"And did she tell you just exactly where in Siena we might find them? Do you have a shop name, an address?"

Frieda frowns. She doesn't like being put her on the spot. "No," she admits, "but she knows they have them."

Firmly I say, "Frieda, we're not going to Siena. We could spend the rest of the day there wandering around looking for *pupi* and not finding any, and you leave tomorrow morning. We have better ways to spend your last day. Why don't you try and find them in Florence on your way back?"

She's about to give in when Vanessa chimes in, "It's not fair we all didn't get what we wanted."

I sigh. "Listen, I'll tell you what I'll do: I'll take everybody's order, and when I come back in a few months, I'll get what you want and bring it all back to the States with me."

Frieda, relieved, sees a way of regaining her popularity. She turns to the group and says, "In that case, I'll give up all my *pupi* to the rest of you, and then all Chef John has to do is replace them for me when he comes back." Everyone is happy and Frieda is much praised; a few women even kiss her, then they all tear into her bag and divide up her purchases.

With our day's itinerary now rescued from having to roar off to Siena for emergency *pupi*-hunting, we continue strolling down the lane, looking into the shops. In an antique store, I see a group of large, striking, oil paintings.

Frieda catches me admiring them and gives them a look. "Those are lovely," she says. "And that's just the shade of blue I love. These would look terrific in my living room. I've even got a bare wall, just perfect for them."

There are four paintings in the group, and the proprietor is willing to separate them. Frieda and I decide to think about purchasing them over lunch.

We choose a sun-soaked outdoor trattoria and order some wonderful aromatic Tuscan antipasti to start. I'm enjoying having a meal where Vanessa and the others aren't expecting me to wait on them hand and foot, and everything seems to be going at just the right, leisurely pace — until Frieda suddenly jumps up and darts away. At first, I think she must have been taken sick, the way she's bolted off.

"Is she okay?" I ask the others.

They all shrug, supremely unconcerned; no one even rises to go after her. I think, *Well, she's your friend, and if you don't care, I'll try not to either.* And I stay put.

Some twenty minutes later, she returns clutching a large parcel, her face beaming with pride. "I bought them!" she chirps. "I bought my paintings!"

I'm a little bit taken aback but I shouldn't be. I've seen Frieda's attack-and-destroy method of shopping already, over the *pupi*. I congratulate her and say, "I think I'll buy one of the other two as well, after lunch."

"Too late," she says, still smiling, as she sits down and scrunches her chair back up to the table. "Another American just took them just as I was getting mine. We were telling each other how lucky we are."

I sigh. So I'm out a painting. Well, there'll be others, and I'll be back again someday. But I have a lingering feeling of having been disrespected again. I can't quite put my finger on it. That's the way it's been all week... these little fleeting discourtesies, petty slights, and haughty remarks. Individually they're not much, but they do add up. Oh yes they do.

That night, as is my habit, I give one final lecture, after which I pass the hat, asking the group to contribute a small gratuity for the dishwasher, a sweet local woman. Anything is acceptable; most people throw in a few dollars, some much more. Personally, I never fail to tip service people, and when I pay our dishwasher I always add in a little gratuity of my own. Then I'll give her the group's tip as well, making sure she knows it's from them. She's very appreciative.

The hat makes its way around the room and most of the women are quite generous. I expect as much; we're Americans, what's a dollar or two to show someone we appreciate her efforts on our behalf?

After the hat returns to me, I distribute an evaluation form for everyone to fill out, to help me understand what they liked and disliked about the week. The goal, of course, is to help me to improve my business. One lady, Sharon, asks if she can take the form home and "really give it some thought," then mail it back to me.

"Of course," I say, grateful she'd devote so much time to the task; "why not?"

After that, the group breaks up for the evening, and everyone begins preparing for their departure in the morning. Most women gather in the living room to wrap their bottles of wine in bubble wrap and otherwise pack their bags for their departure the next day. I'm in the living room as well, but apart from the women, reading a book. Every so often I'll make an effort to join in their conversation, but I'm always coolly rebuffed. So I keep reading and eventually retire to bed. I'm quite happy to see the last of this group, and I'm certain the feeling is mutual.

On Friday morning we have our last class together. We're making a large batch of coconut cookies. One of the women pats her stomach and says, "We should only make a few. We've already eaten so much this week."

"Let's go ahead and make them anyway," I suggest. "You can either take them with you to eat later, or I can give them to Albarosa".

"That'd be great," someone says. "Make the whole batch, and you take her what's left over with our compliments." There's general agreement; Albarosa has some fans here.

So we proceed with our original plan. The cookies come out wonderfully moist and aromatic, and melt in our mouths. After everyone's had their fill of them, I take what's left and arrange them on a platter that I'll run over to Albarosa this afternoon, once I've returned from dropping the women off in Florence.

The class ends, final preparations for departure are seen to and soon we're packing the car with the women's luggage. Before leaving, I make one last circuit of the house to make sure no one has left anything behind, and that all the doors are locked. I find Vanessa in the kitchen, stuffing the leftover cookies into a bag.

"What are you doing? " I cry. "I had those all arranged to take to Albarosa! That was the decision of the group!"

She gives me a who-are-you-to-question-me look and says, "Well, *my* decision is that I need them more than she does." She almost snorts in disgust at my presumption, then turns and walks out to the van. Haughty and self-righteous to the end, that one.

At the Florence train station I see them all off. Frieda reminds me of my promise to fill her *pupi* order, and Vanessa shakes my hand with all the warmth of a vampire, and then they're off — and I am blissfully alone. The week is over, these women can't kick me around anymore.

Or so I think.

A month after I return to Atlanta, I get Sharon's evaluation in the mail. For the most part, she has only glowing things to say about her week with me. She learned a lot, she acquired new skills, etcetera. Something in her tone, however, tells me a "but" is coming...

I'm right. She loved the whole experience, *but* she didn't appreciate me passing a hat for the dishwasher. That, she writes, was uncalled for and unprofessional and as a matter of fact she'd like her five dollars back.

I write out a check for five dollars and send it to Sharon with a note kindly thanking her for taking such time and care over her responses. It's a real masterpiece of hiding what I really want to say.

People never stop surprising me. To think that a woman like Sharon — educated, privileged, affluent — can let something as petty as a five dollar tip for a lowly service person get in her gut and fester there!

It isn't long before I realize I've let *her* get into *my* gut. So I de-

cide that from now on I won't distribute these evaluation forms anymore. It almost seems to be asking people to find something to complain about. And really, I don't need them. I give the people a highly
memorable week, with fantastic meals accompanied with outstand-
ing wines, and scenic side trips to places they wouldn't venture to on
their own. I don't want to hear about a lousy five dollar tip. My students get their money's worth. If they don't feel that's the case, they
can tell me. I usually know how things are going by the mood of the
house and the level of laughter and conversation in the van. I don't
need evaluation forms.

Nowadays I send out a questionnaire *before* the trip, which is returned to me with payment for the week. This lets me learn in advance anything I might need to know — such as any food allergies or
physical disabilities that will have to be accommodated during the
week. I also ask what expectations students have for their time with
me. That, too, is something that helps me tailor my agenda for each
group. It also helps me weed out problems — for instance, I actively
discourage vegetarians from signing on. I used to think that there's
enough food prepared at every meal for non-meat-eaters to enjoy and
not to have to worry about everyone filling up. But some vegetarians
don't eat any eggs or cheese, either. And that can create a problem.
Sometimes having to make an additional dish or sauce.

Now, I don't pass judgment on vegetarians. I don't eat much meat
myself. It can be hard to digest. But I like eating cheeses in Europe
because they don't pasteurize the milk they're made from. Therefore
the cheeses have an actual life, and they price and sell cheeses by
their age. It's amazing the profound difference age can make in the
taste and texture of the same type of cheese. When I'm in Europe I
serve cheese a lot, and often cheese is an ingredient in the dishes I
cook as well. So for someone to ask — as one woman once did — that
everything containing cheese be eliminated, it makes things very difficult for me. Since the other students won't agree to give up cheese
or eggs, this means I essentially plan two separate menus. It would
be different if I had a *whole group* of vegetarians; that might be a
challenge, a reason to push myself and come up with some really inventive recipes for the week. But so far, no one's ever proposed that.

Now, years after these events, I've learned to "read" groups better; certainly I've never misread one as badly as I did Vanessa and her friends. But even that group has surprised me. Several of its members have returned to study with me in Europe again, coming back to Tuscany with a different group of friends. Or with a group of couples, eager to show them the Tuscany they saw years earlier with me. I've never actually cornered any of them to ask what went wrong with their original tour — Southern women don't answer direct questions, remember — deciding instead to just be grateful that I'd misinterpreted their earlier displeasure.

Even Frieda returned to my cooking classes in Atlanta. Frieda, whose order for *pupi* I dutifully filled, and delivered to her on my next return from Italy. Frieda, who was delighted to have her collection restored in this way. Frieda, of whom all I asked was that she repay the money I'd spent on her behalf. Of course she never has. Even after several phone calls and a letter requesting the money I spent on her behalf. Though she'll blithely take new students into my teaching kitchen, show them my chef *pupo*, explain what it is and where they come from and even brag about her own collection.

Have I mentioned that people surprise me?... Anyway, onward.

quattro

The Name Game

DURING THE WEEK MY STUDENTS SPEND WITH ME, we often have down time in the evenings after our intensive days of planned activities. Actually, as both the chef and the owner of the business, I usually don't have much unscheduled time myself. But as my students do, I make it a point to spend it with them, to provide some structure and direction and make certain they keep enjoying themselves. And most people do need direction, since their default activity — watching television — is a letdown here, since everything is in Italian, leaving them at a loss for what to do. And idle hands are the devil's workshop, as they say.

So I opt for getting everyone involved in games. This brings everyone together as a community, increases camaraderie, and melts away any leftover stress from the day in warm, convivial laughter. This is particularly useful when a student is having trouble getting along with the group. Such a student is with me now. Her name is Kathleen, a rather timid middle-aged woman who seems to have lived a sheltered life. She has trouble following the rapid-fire conversations in the kitchen, and often has to ask people to repeat themselves, which the others are reluctant to do since it interrupts the rhythm of their chatter. As a result, she's become something of an outsider, and she clearly feels it.

Several years ago I was introduced to The Name Game at a friend's Christmas party and it's proven to be a perennial favorite among Culinary Vacations students. Here's a short rundown on how it works:

Everyone is given the name of a famous person — dead or alive, male or female. The name is written on a Post-It note and stuck to your forehead so that you can't see whose name you've been assigned. The object of the game is to guess who you are by asking the minimum number of yes-or-no questions to the other players. Once we have a winner we usually go on until everyone has guessed who they are, in the interest of good sportsmanship. After all, it's only a game and we're here to have fun!

The hilarity often starts before we even start playing. In fact, there are usually laughs as I walk around the dining room table (where we're all seated for easy viewing), and stick a name to each person's forehead. This is because I sometimes choose celebrities who resemble the student in question, or who share the same voice or accent. Tonight there's much merriment because I've given a short, wisecracking fellow named Reuben the name of Billy Crystal.

The rules are simple (they have to be; the point is to relax after a hard day of sight seeing). Each player takes a turn asking a single question to the others. We continue around the table this way until someone makes the right deduction, at which time we all applaud.

The questions begin. Generally they're very broad, to help the narrowing-down process. "Am I male?" "Am I alive?" "Am I in politics?" — and so on. Then we get to Reuben. His first question is, "Do I host a daytime talk show with Regis Philbin?" The others crack up and tell him *no*.

Eventually we get to Kathleen. She looks a little excited but also a little frightened, as though eager to play but still not quite certain of how. We all grow quiet as we await her first question. The silence seems to unnerve her, and she blurts the first thing that comes to her mind — which is apparently still back in the kitchen:

"Am I a chef?"

Fortunately, I often do give people the names of celebrity chefs, on the assumption that as cooking students they'll be easily familiar with them. (I always try to choose famous people whom everyone will know. It's no fun if the names are too obscure or difficult to guess.) In this case, I've given Kathleen the name of Emeril Lagasse.

Everyone shouts *"Yes!"* and Kathleen almost rises out of her chair in surprise. She smiles for the first time — she's happy! I feel a sense of *mission: accomplished.*

Unfortunately, she can't seem to get any farther than that. Her succeeding questions are good ones — "Am I on TV?" "Am I famous for a certain kind of food?" — but soon everyone else has succeeding in guessing their names, and we're still waiting for Kathleen, whose questions are getting lamer ("Do I have brown hair?") and she still hasn't offered up a single guess. Not Jamie Oliver, not Rachael Ray, not the Barefoot Contessa — nobody.

People are starting to get a little tense, so I decide to break the rules and offer Kathleen extra clues. I lean across the table and say, *"BAM!"*

She's clearly not prepared for this and almost tips over in her chair from shock.

Now we're back to square one with an intimidated Kathleen and an impatient everyone else. In my most jovial voice I declare the first ever Name Game stumper, and tell Kathleen she may remove her sticker and read her name aloud.

She plucks the note from her forehead... looks at it... and after a long pause says, "I don't know how to pronounce this."

We're all flabbergasted. It turns out Kathleen has never watched the Food Network or Food TV. She's never seen, or even heard of Sara Moulton, Alton Brown, the Two Fat Ladies, or anybody else. But come on. I don't even own a television and I know Emeril.

We all stare at her for a while and then — fortunately — we all start to laugh, Kathleen as well. We laugh long and hard, and by the time we're all done, Kathleen is part of the gang.

When the last of the laughter has faded Kathleen says, "But... I still don't know how to pronounce it," and that sets us right off again.

Sometimes the roles assumed for The Name Game stick for the rest of the week. "Oh, Nigella! What beautiful pasta sauce you are making!" "Thank you, Chopin, I call it my Symphony Sauce after you, my dear..." And so on. And sure enough, for the rest of the week Kathleen is playfully called "Emeril."

But everyone deliberately mispronounces it.

5

cinque

The Woman I Almost Sent Home

EVERY GROUP IS DIFFERENT. This one is made up of two sisters-in-law, Beth and Mary, their friend Priscilla, Priscilla's friends Pat and Dorothy and three other women variously connected with them. Eight people in all — the maximum number I'll accept — unless someone wants to rent a car and stay outside the villa. I have the rooms I can book for such an eventuality. But with more than eight, it does get tight in the kitchen.

All the women are dressed in black when I meet them at the train station. All Southerners, sweet and genteel. "Nahce to meet you, Chef," they say — that charming Dixie lilt. Butter wouldn't melt. Even so, I'm on my guard: I know the habit of some Southern women to smile and say nothing when they really want to complain or, worse, go into a rage. I think they hold it all in. Or they're in deep denial about the way things really are.

When I studied psychology years ago, I learned quite a bit about this word *denial*. Suppressing reality, looking through rose colored glasses — that's it in a nutshell. Having gone to school in New York, I like to get it all out. Whatever it is, let's bring it into the open and thrash it out. Find out what needs fixing, then fix it, get on with things and everything will be fine. I'm okay, you're okay.

After nine years in this business, you become a swift judge of character, adept at ferreting out what people are like and, more importantly, what they want from you. I've learned a lot since I started out. When I began, I assumed that Culinary Vacations students were like the college students I've taught; that they'd come to me to learn something, and if they didn't learn it they'd risk failing. But it's different with Culinary Vacations. People come here for a variety of reasons. In fact that list is very lengthy.

So I've relaxed in my style of teaching. I teach people what they want to learn, or what they're able to learn, instead of sticking to a rigid program and insisting that everybody get everything right. *Did I say lower my standards?*

A Culinary Vacation day begins with everyone gathering in the living room for a lecture. I go over the itinerary for the day, the menu, and the recipes. I assign the recipes, usually to teams of two students. It's their responsibility to complete their assignment during class, after which we assemble the full meal and serve it buffet style, accompanied by local wines. That way, we all enjoy what we've cooked. Each day the menu changes, and so do the cooking partners. So if you're working on dessert today, tomorrow you might be preparing the main course — with a new colleague at your side.

If there's a particular cooking technique I want to get across to the group, I use the lecture as the opportunity to explain and demonstrate for them. I go carefully over each recipe so that everyone has an understanding of what will be going on in the kitchen for the day. Sometimes students want to watch another group as they tackle a certain step in their assignment. There's always time to observe others while working on your own recipe. I oversee the entire cooking process and assist when needed, keeping everyone on the right path.

During my first lecture with the Southern ladies, I assign Beth a recipe: orange cake with orange glaze. She smiles and nods, seemingly confident. But during the actual cooking class, I detect a lot of frozen smiles from Beth and her partner, Dorothy. Something's wrong, but being Southern they're madly suppressing it. Unfortunately I'm busy helping another student through an intricate part of her own recipe, and I have no time to investigate.

Later, Dorothy catches me alone. "Chef," she says, "I hate to speak ill of anybody." Southern women always start their complaints with a disclaimer about how they never complain. "But I have to tell you, that Beth is a mess! She was completely unorganized and had no idea what she was doing, so I had to take over the whole job myself before she ruined it. Then she put her nose in the air like I'd offended her or something. I was a nervous wreck by the time we finished. I won't have to work with her again, will I?"

I reassure her that, with eight students, there are plenty of combinations available so that she won't get saddled with Beth again before the week is up. I apologize for the difficulty, and she leaves happy.

Then I turn my mind to Beth. She's a diminutive lady — only about 5′2″ —with shoulder-length, frosted hair, beautiful green eyes, in her late thirties, early forties. A small-town girl from Georgia. You'd look at her and think, "What a darling!" But as I said, I know Southern women. And those petite little frames can contain the heart of a raging lion.

I decide to do nothing for now. Possibly Beth's only problem was that she didn't mesh well with Dorothy. So for the next class I pair her with Pat, and assign them a Primavera pasta sauce, which is a bit more complex and requires a lot of slicing and dicing. Beth and Pat get started chopping; I'm keeping an eye on them. They seem to be having a little trouble, and are wasting a lot of time and food. I step in and suggest that they hold the knife in a certain manner, and cut the peppers julienne style, like so.

A while later I return and show them how to mince cloves of garlic. We then proceed to the peeling and slicing of the onion. It becomes a knife skills class. In my opinion, if you don't know how to cut vegetables you're really making it hard for yourself. I always suggest a knife skills class as a prerequisite for anyone. Knowing which blade to use and how to use it gets you out of the kitchen much faster, and efficiency is vital when you're cooking. But in the meantime, I'm spending a lot of time with Beth and Pat, while trying to give a fair amount to the other students as well, as we all work together on our luncheon.

The effort is worth it. At mealtime the students all bring their completed courses to the table and present them. And we enjoy a fantastic lunch with a few bottles of mellow regional wine.

It's now Monday afternoon. We have an appointment at a winery for a tour and tasting. We clean up, pile in the van, and travel to town to soak up the local atmosphere (and of course to shop), then head over to the vineyard. Everyone's happy, enjoying themselves — but in the rearview mirror I can see that frozen smile on Beth's face again. She isn't speaking, isn't joining in. Something's roiling inside of her, but she's putting up quite a front. I wonder how long before it collapses.

Not long, as it happens. We return to the villa in early evening, and as we head up the driveway to the villa the women announce that they're heading to their rooms for a short nap while I prepare dinner. This is fine with me; it's been a long day and they've done well. They've earned a little rest.

I'm in the kitchen greasing a pan when Beth appears in the doorway. The frozen smile is gone, replaced by a dark frown.

"Hey there, Beth," I say carefully. "What can I do for you?"

"Chef, I'm sorry I have to say this" — there's the disclaimer — "but I really feel you've been picking on me during class."

I'm astonished. "Really?"

"Yes, really," she says. "And it's upset me."

I put down the pan. "I'm sorry you feel that way, Beth. I'd never deliberately single anyone out. I'm here to teach you about cooking, that's all, and I don't *think* I've treated you any differently than I have anyone else. Your recipe was pretty complicated, so possibly I spent more time watching over you..."

"And calling attention to it," she says, her face reddening. Her Southern reserve is evaporating.

"Is that what you think?... Beth, when I tell you how to do something, it makes sense that everyone else hears it too. That way, you all learn together. That's my only goal here. I want every one of you to acquire a new set of skills and techniques while you're here with me in Tuscany."

"Well, you act like I've never cooked before," she says. "For God's sake, I raised four boys, how do you think I got food on the table?" I want to say, *Not by julienning peppers, that's for sure,* but I wisely keep this thought to myself. Seriously, I'm astonished to hear that she's been cooking for years. Maybe she's counting the frozen dinners she's heated in the microwave. Because she is as close to a beginner as anyone I've ever taught.

Now that the dam has burst, there's no stopping the flow of Beth's anger. She tells me she doesn't like the way I'm singling her out, and she wants it all to stop, immediately. I tell her I'm sorry, but I thought that she was here to learn. A bit more of this back-and-forth — by now I'm a little upset myself — and she concludes with a damning, "I thought this was supposed to be fun — well, *I'm* not having fun," and storms off to her room.

I'm left standing there, rather stunned, still gripping my greased pan. What just happened? I replay the whole conversation in my head. I try to be fair. Was I maybe too hard on her? Was it possible I really did pick on her more than anyone else? I'm in a quandary. What do I do now?

Glumly I proceed with fixing dinner, hoping this doesn't put a damper on the rest of the group. I hope there's not a flurry of discussion going on behind my back. The way the house is designed, the kitchen and the bedrooms are at opposite ends. There could be a systematic analysis of everything I've done and said going on, and I wouldn't even know it.

I finish the dinner and call everyone to the table. I get some strange looks as they enter the dining room. I don't know what to make of them.

Beth is conspicuously absent. Her best friend Priscilla and her sister-in-law Mary appear to know what's going on. And the others, if they haven't already figured it out, are now to find out. Mary proceeds to tell me that Beth isn't coming out of her room for the rest of the week. Now, I've tried to be fair to her, but this strikes me as just plain childish. *Fine, let her starve,* I find myself thinking.

Instead I shrug my shoulders and say, "I'm sorry, I'm not sure what I've done wrong."

Mary says, "No, I can imagine you aren't. I never am when this happens to me." I give her a startled look, and she smiles and adds, "Let's just say Beth's a little immature. We have problems like this all the time with her."

Priscilla reaches over and pats my arm consolingly. "Listen," she says, "I have to travel with her because our husbands are brothers and they want us to be good friends. Well, we aren't. I had to be persuaded to bring her here, against my better judgment, and look what's happened. And this is just the second day!"

I'm grateful for all this support. And I'm thinking, if this woman really is such a disruptive influence, let me just get through tomorrow; then on Wednesday I can take her back to Florence and plunk her butt on a train, any train, who cares where it's headed. As long as she's out of my hair, right?

The rest of the meal passes pleasantly enough. Then it's Tuesday morning and time for another cooking class. Beth is still a no-show and I'm still the bad guy — at least, that's how it feels. Someone takes Beth a plate of food for lunch — the same woman who, apparently, took her a tray of dinner last night, which she refused to eat. Well, I wouldn't eat either after insulting a talented chef whose only crime is showing me right from wrong in the kitchen. But I doubt those were her reasons.

After class we're are scheduled to go to a small winery owned by a father and daughter. The father's name is Carlo, and he likes women a lot. I figure, if I can somehow get Beth to accompany us on this tour, Carlo will work his charm on her and everything will be back to normal. And if not?... Then it's back to my earlier plan, and back she goes to the Florence train station.

I go to her room to try and knock. "Beth?... It's Chef John. May I please speak with you?"

After a rather long pause, she opens the door a crack, as though I might try to force my way in. *Honestly.* I swallow my pride and once again apologize, telling her I'd like to get back on track for the rest of the week. And that I'd like very much for her to join us on our excursion this afternoon, as I'm sure she'd enjoy it.

"Oh, no," she says, as if I've wounded her too deeply for even the possibility of ever enjoying herself again.

"Beth," I say, "you've paid for this trip. You're in Italy. This is all once-in-a-lifetime! Just come out with us and see the Tuscan scenery. You can't miss that. And who knows, you might even like this winery. The views from the terrace are breathtaking." I pause. "And then, if you want to spend the rest of the week in your room, well, you can."

In the end, she condescends to go with us on our outing. She appears in a little black dress and sandals, her hair pulled back in a knot. She looks fabulous. I smile, thinking of Carlo's reaction.

Sure enough, when we arrive at the vineyard, Carlo makes a bee-line for her and turns on his charm. I don't even have to ask him. He asks the *bella signora* for permission to take her arm as he shows her the winery, and of course Beth giggles and agrees. And from then on he treats her like a queen, giving her the first taste of every wine and waiting for her reaction before pouring a glass for anyone else. She visibly melts at all this fawning attention.

By the time we return to the villa, Beth is acting as if nothing has happened between us, and we finish our week in Tuscany splendidly. Which is a fine thing. Because I wasn't relishing the idea of that forty minute drive to Florence alone in the van with her. No sir, I was not.

6
sei

A Short History of Tuscany

MUCH HAS CHANGED since I first arrived in this region over eight years ago. This countryside seems so serene and eternal, that any alteration is immediately apparent, and surprising. But it has changed, and in fundamental ways

On that initial visit, I was scouting for a location for my classes. I was looking for a small city, with lots of charm and a unique atmosphere that offered sufficient amenities and attractions for my students — all within reasonable driving distance of the locations we'd be visiting during the week. So I drove great distances, in the process discovering many small villages and towns. I was able to get a feel for the place in a relatively short time.

Everywhere I went I saw large farmhouses, many, if not most of them abandoned, their windows dark and gaping. Now, some eight years later, you can't find many empty houses. They've all been snapped up by wealthy Americans and Europeans who have restored them and now either rent them out or use them as holiday homes.

Tuscany is a rich region. In fact I'm told there are no poor in Tuscany. Its vineyards, olive orchards, and leather factories are enough to guarantee a certain level of prosperity. But when you factor in tourism, it goes right off the charts. You can easily imagine the potential to make a very good living among these rolling hills.

Tuscan chic has almost become a cottage industry in this country. It seems every time you turn around, another American has moved here to experience the Tuscan way of life firsthand, then written a best selling novel or memoir about his or her experiences. And this is just fine with me. The more interest there is in Tuscany, the more my business continues to grow.

And there seems no chance the level of interest will wane anytime soon. The curious still flock here to see the fabled land for themselves and have their own unforgettable experiences. You can't blame them. Tuscany is so ravishingly beautiful, with its Cypress-strewn hills, acres of grape vines, silvery olive trees, and noble deciduous hardwoods. In spring the iris blooms in multiple shades of purple, complemented by the bracing yellow of Lady Banks roses climbing the pine trees. Wild fig trees dot the landscape, their limbs bearing rich wine-colored fruit, ripe for the picking along the roadside.

When fall comes, the cold snaps the trees and the colors change overnight. I find it similar to experiencing autumn in the northern United States. And what a bounty of treasures it brings! Chestnut trees groan with innumerable fruits; wild fennel erupts, aromatic and ready to harvest; mushrooms of seemingly infinite names and varieties scatter across the woodlands. Hunting season begins, for birds of all kinds and for Tuscany's famous wild boar. And of course there's the grape harvest, with each village hosting its own splendid wine festival. A very busy season to be in Tuscany, and my favorite time of the year in Italy.

Tuscany hasn't always been so prosperous. After World War II, the soldiers came home and tried to rebuild their lives and make a living. The soil was tilled to grow fruits and vegetables, and the government established a new law giving sharecroppers money from the land barons so that all could profit from the harvest.

But the soil wasn't the right composition for growing vegetables. So the yield was nil, and the landowners had no profit to share. So many Tuscans pulled up stakes and left to find a better life elsewhere, simply abandoning their humble homes. It's hard to conceive of the beautiful countryside of Tuscany being essentially empty, but in essence, it was. When news of this migration spread, canny city dwellers arrived to buy up the abandoned land as vacation spots for next to nothing. Entire villages were purchased for a song — just so people could rid themselves of property they no longer wanted and presumed to be worthless.

After the disastrous experiment with other crops, the countryside was slowly but surely replanted with the grapevines and olive trees for which it has historically been renowned. Nature knew best all along; the soil is perfectly suited for grow thousands of hectares of these products, and has helped turn the area into a hugely profitable wine and olive oil industry.

In the early days of Chianti production, the manufacture of this popular wine was unregulated and as a result many inferior bottles damaged its reputation. Americans today can still remember the straw-covered bottles that became synonymous with cheapness in wine from Italy. It's taken forty years of legislation and public relations to change the minds of the public, but today Chianti Classico is a respected and popular brand, unlike its ancestor of fifty years ago.

Today Tuscany is producing many new wines as well, using new and innovative blends of grapes. These red table wines were dubbed Super Tuscans by the wine guru Robert Parker, and they're making another huge profit for the Tuscans of today.

In short, it's a kind of golden age in Tuscany though we shouldn't lose sight of the years of labor, suffering, and loss that made it all possible. Indeed, knowledge of this past makes the present riches seem even sweeter.

sette

"I Only Came To Get Away From My Husband"

I'M PUTTING TOGETHER A GROUP of women for a week in Tuscany in August. I don't usually schedule trips for summer, but I'm always happy to customize a special tour at any time my schedule will permit me to return to Europe.

This particular trip will bring me to Tuscany about three weeks earlier than I would normally arrive. I'm hoping it won't be a very hot summer — one of those sizzlers that go down in the record books. But even if it is, there's a silver lining: after the trip concludes, I won't have to return home, since it will be just two weeks till the beginning of my regular cooking tour in mid-September, when the weather cools a bit and the majority of tourists depart. Having two weeks off in Tuscany will be a dream. I'll be able to reacquaint myself with my favorite haunts, work on my book, even cook for friends. Maybe the family will come over for a visit.

This particular trip is being organized at the request of a new client named Madge. She saw an article about my cooking tours in The Atlanta Journal one cold day in February, when the thought of warm ovens in sun-kissed Tuscany must have been irresistible. She clipped out the article and vowed, "One day I'm going to do that." A woman of her word, eighteen months later she called to request a customized week. She wanted to include her daughter, who's already abroad, having taken a job in southern Italy. They're both eager to learn to prepare Italian cuisine, and where better than the country that invented it?... I told Madge that's great, but I need more than two persons for a group. She immediately began canvassing her friends to get them to join her on this adventure.

Unfortunately, she's not having much luck. So far no one has signed on. Just about every day or so Madge phones or emails me with a new set of people who she's just remembered might want to join her. "Send them a brochure!" she'll say, as if the idea might not otherwise occur to me. Of course I'll send a brochure. For me to commit to this customized week, I'll have to have at least four people enrolled, and would love to reach my eight-student maximum. August is high season, when my costs are much greater, so it's vital we get this settled as soon as possible.

Madge's lists of friends become longer and longer — wave after wave of Sylvias, Barbaras, Tinas, Nancys — but no one is signing up. Finally she decides to call them all, one by one, to ask them point-blank whether they're interested. She reports back to me a little later: "I don't understand," she says, nervous laughter coloring her voice, "no one seems to know a thing about a cooking school in Tuscany. Are you sure you sent those brochures?"

I assure Madge that my hands are near cramped from all the envelope stuffing I've done daily, at her behest. And checking my notes, it seems that there's been more than enough time for the brochures to have reached their recipients. Thirty in all. Without a single response. The only explanation I can think of, is that Madge's friends must have taken the brochure for junk mail and disposed of it without looking at it.

I send out a fresh batch, to the entire thirty-person list, with *Sent to you by Madge* written on the envelopes. I hope this does the trick. But after a few days, we still have no confirmations beyond Madge and her daughter.

No confirmations, and no money.

Madge remains certain that she can get a group together. Cost isn't an issue; these women are affluent, accustomed to travel. And Madge reassures me that some of them are indeed interested in joining her. It's just a matter of nailing them down. These are busy women, she tells me; always active, always running off somewhere, juggling three things at once.

Something drastic must be done. I need deposits to secure spaces for the week, and I need them very soon. Madge is a sweet lady, but it seems her organizational skills aren't quite up to the task. It's time for me to take over.

Often when a group expresses interest in going to Europe with me, I have its members to dinner at my house. It's a good way for everyone to meet and break the ice — and, of course, persuade any fence sitters of my *bona fides*. Madge's group is *all* fence sitters, and I'm not certain everyone she's invited knows everyone else; and I of course haven't met any of them — not even Madge. So a dinner seems like the ideal solution. We can all get together, relax, and over a shared meal I can answer any questions they may have. Also, a little fine wine will help them make any inquiries they might've been too shy to broach otherwise. In my experience, it's rare that such a dinner ends without a few new recruits producing their checkbooks before departing.

Of course, these dinners aren't without their inherent risks. A few years ago I hosted a group of twelve ladies, some of whom were interested in joining me for cooking lessons, but were hesitant to commit. For that dinner, I pulled out all the stops. I knew for a fact that within the group there were some women who were already accomplished cooks, and I wanted to reassure them that I could indeed take them to a higher level. So I prepared my signature Cassoulet.

It turned out wonderfully, possibly the best I'd ever made — full of flavor, the meats tender and juicy — with no fat floating on top, the way the French serve it. My cassoulet is an American slant on the traditional recipe, and far less fatty. I complemented it with a nice, crisp salad with several toppings, and an assortment of homemade dressings. For dessert, something chocolate was called for. Women love chocolate.

The cassoulet was a great success — in fact, too much so. Everyone at the table wanted the recipe. One woman in particular was insistent. As she bore down on me, my hand crept instinctively towards my salad fork. Who knew, I might need a weapon to keep her at bay. "If you'd like the recipe," I said calmly and firmly, "you'll have to come with me to Provence."

Unfortunately, the group was scheduled for Tuscany. "Couldn't we learn it there?"

"They don't serve cassoulet in Tuscany," I explained to howls of protest. The ugly scene eventually wound down, but the dinner never quite regained an amicable footing. The women just couldn't — or wouldn't — realize that this is my business. I sell recipes to make my living. I can't just give them away, gratuitously.

Anyway, I have higher hopes for Madge's group. Madge and I agree on a date, invitations go out, and nine of her friends accept. With Madge and myself, that makes eleven. I round out the table by inviting a former client, Susan, who lives in the Atlanta area and who has attended all of my cooking school locations. She promises to bring her photo album, filled with laughing, happy people and gorgeous Tuscan landscapes, and to make herself available to answer any questions that may require a woman's point of view. I figure I now have all my bases covered.

Usually for such a dinner I prepare a light meal, like a salad and a large pasta dish with my fresh-baked focaccia bread, and a simple but very good chocolate dessert. (Again, chocolate is crucial.) But at the last minute I decide to serve Coq au Vin instead. I have all the ingredients already in the fridge, it'll be a snap to bring them all together, and the dish will be impressive. It's not Italian, but the women will be getting plenty of that in Italy. At least I hope.

Then at the eleventh hour, a cancellation. There's a momentary flash of impending doom, but I manage to quell it. "She probably wasn't a serious recruit anyway," I tell myself. But the fact remains: we're down to eight. I've got to do my best to sell them the trip. I need at least four of them signed up by the end of the evening.

I get tied up at the office and don't get home until very late. I'd wanted to straighten up the house a bit and have everything ready for when the women arrive, but I guess it'll have to be more of an informal evening. I get to work in the kitchen, and have just started on the Coq au Vin when the doorbell rings. *Damn*, I think, *someone's on time.*

I answer the door and admit a tall, formidable looking lady in a pink jacket with a purse so large I think she must have packed for the trip already. She introduces herself as Cathy. I pour her a glass of red wine and set her on a stool in the kitchen and get back to the Coq au

Vin. Cathy wants me to tell her a little about the wine she's drinking, so I have to talk while I'm cooking but soon she interrupts me to talk about herself, which is very helpful. I listen with one ear, and focus more attention on preparing dinner.

Fortunately, I have everything well in hand by the time the other guests arrive, along with Madge, who's a pleasant, wide-eyed woman who seems a little overwhelmed by what she's set in motion. Everyone talks around her; she seems always a sentence behind everyone else.

I've had to do a bit of scrambling, but everyone is in a good mood, chatting and laughing and sipping their wine, so there's no awkwardness about having to, say, fetch a chair from another room. And really, the food has come out perfectly, and for an event like this, that's the only important thing, right?

Before dinner we all sit around the island in my kitchen, where I've arranged an impressive array of appetizers and several wine selections. We begin a lively discussion about the week and what it has to offer. I have several copies of the itinerary, which I distribute so that the women can see just exactly what they'd be doing with me each day.

They examine these as they finish their first glasses of wine, then pore over Susan's photo album with their second. It's all going very well, lots of chatter and enthusiasm and Susan is wonderfully effusive about her own experiences. By the time we sit down to dinner everyone seems relaxed and happy. And when the Coq au Vin comes out, there are oohs and aahs of appreciation. I feel I've got them exactly where I want them.

But do I?... The always delicate question of cost comes up. I explain again that the price reflects the reality of being in Italy during the high season. "The country will be choked with tourists," I say, "and as a result everything will cost double." For some women, this is a hurdle they can't quite clear. Others are blithely unconcerned about price. It becomes clear that, while none of the women lack money, some have quite a bit more to spend than others.

Then Cathy puts down her wine glass and says, "August in Italy. I don't know. How hot do you think it will be?" Her tone of voice indicates that she, for one, thinks it will be very hot indeed.

"Honestly," I say, "I've never been to Tuscany in August. I don't run trips during the summer for several reasons. Price is certainly one of them and I have to admit heat is another. And there's really no air-conditioning in Europe."

"Oh, my," says a fair-skinned woman named Mary, her head jerking up as though I'd just said there was no plumbing.

"But Madge is game," I say, nodding to Madge, who at the moment suddenly doesn't look game at all, "and this is the only opening I have for a private group for several months. I'm sure we'll all be fine."

Cathy doesn't say anything, but she looks very dubious, as though I were a snake-oil salesman. I'm thinking she's not going to commit; women of her sort don't like to endure any kind of inconvenience — especially something like summer heat, which no one can be sued for.

Pam, a tall woman with a very severe haircut and glasses so thick they're almost opaque, asks about the meals we'll be preparing during the week. "Are they the classic Italian dishes or are they your own creations?" The slight emphasis she puts on the last three words isn't entirely flattering, but I choose to rise above it.

"A little of both," I say. "They're seasonal recipes based on what the Tuscan region produces at that time of year. So yes, we'll get a little bit inventive with them, but we'll certainly prepare the classics as well." I've learned from experience that most of my students want to get the classics under their belts.

"If I were to come in spite of the heat," says Cathy suddenly, "I'd like a room with a private bath."

Of course she would. "I'm sorry," I say, "that's already taken." I don't add that Madge and her daughter have claimed it, to spare Madge the pressure of offering it up as a sacrifice. "All I have left are rooms with shared baths."

"As long as we learn the classics," Pam says suddenly. "Like osso buco."

"Well, that's more of a winter dish," I say. "But we'll see what's in the markets when we get there."

"I really can't share a bathroom," says Cathy. "There must be something you can do."

I shrug. "There's also the living room, where I usually sleep; that has a private bathroom, but you'd have to sleep on a pull-out sofa bed." Cathy looks as though I've just sentenced her to hard labor.

Pam is sulking now. "No osso buco?"

A heavyset woman named Linda speaks up. "I might like the living room, actually," she says. "So Denise and I don't have to sleep in the same bed."

"Oh, yes," says Denise, who's a larger gal herself. "That's a good idea."

A willowy, red-faced blond named Mary, who's perhaps had a touch too much to drink, says, "I don't care if we cook osso buco or Chef Boy-Ar-Dee, I'm just interested in getting away from my husband."

"Me, too," says a waiflike woman named Emma.

"But, if Linda sleeps in the living room," says Denise, her brow furrowed, "who's going to be my roommate?"

"Actually, there are two sofa beds in the living room," I say, while Mary and Emma start talking between themselves about their husbands. "You can take the other one, and you and Linda can still be together."

"Does that open up a room with a bath?" asks Cathy.

"No," I say, as Mary and Emma's conversation gets louder and merrier. I feel like I'm losing control of the group. No one seems entirely contented at the moment, except the two women who don't want to cook and aren't listening to me anyway.

I clear my throat, and Mary and Emma take the hint, sitting up straight and giving me their attention. But they continue to laugh.

Cathy takes Mary's arm and says, "My friend Missy and I will share a room." Clearly she thinks she'd better act fast before Mary bonds too firmly with Emma.

"What about goulash?" asks Pam.

I blink. "What?"

"Will we be learning goulash?"

"Um... that's Hungarian."

"No, the Italian kind."

I blink again. "I... don't know what you mean."

"Isn't there any way Mary and I can get a private bath?" Cathy asks again. She's clearly not the kind of woman who takes no for an answer.

"I think she means risotto," says Madge, looking at Pam.

"That's it!" Pam cries.

I'm about to retort that goulash and risotto are nothing alike, but I catch myself and say, "Yes, we can make risotto." Now I have Cathy clearing her throat at *me*.

I sigh, turn to her, and say, "Well, there is one other option. There's an apartment next door with a private bath. You'd have to pay a little more for it, to cover my added expenditure."

Cathy grimaces at this but appears to be thinking it over.

Meanwhile Pam has been glaring at Mary and Emma. "I only want to come if this is a serious cooking course," she says. "I for one am *not* going just to get away from my husband, and I don't want the lessons to be ruined by people who aren't there to cook."

"Oh, we'll cook!" cries Emma, and Mary tries to hide a laugh. "I mean, I mainly want to get away from George, but I really do like to cook, and that's why I'm considering a cooking vacation."

Pam nods and says, "Well, all right then."

"Also, the scenery and shopping," Emma adds, which only makes Pam frown again.

"I'm definitely coming for the cooking," says Madge with gusto. "But I'm just getting over hip replacement surgery so I have to be able to sit down while I cook. That's not going to be a problem, is it?"

At this, Pam almost gets up and leaves the table. A woman named Norma puts a hand on her shoulder and says, "*I'm* serious about the cooking, hon. And I mean serious. I've taken courses at the Cordon Bleu. In *Paris*."

Mary chooses this untimely moment to laugh again, and Norma's hackles raise up.

Things seem to be dissolving. I give Madge a look. These are her friends, she should step in to bring them back together.

She takes my cue and says, "Well, my daughter and I just think it's great to learn about Italian cooking in Italy, especially because she lives there now. But her job hasn't left her any time to learn the cuisine. So this is the ideal week for both of us, and I do hope some of you will make it all possible by joining us."

There's a moment of silence, and I think Madge has pulled it off. Then Cathy puts her elbow on the table, leans in, and says, "Let me get this straight: your daughter who lives in Italy is going to spend her vacation in Italy learning Italian cooking from an American?"

I quickly decide it's time for the chocolate.

I was right. The dark, luscious dessert restores order and harmony to the table. And by the end of the night Pam, Norma, Mary, and Cathy have confirmed that they're in, and have written me checks. Which brings the total to eight with Madge and her daughter, and two coming from out of town who want private rooms with private baths.

After the guests have all gone, I think back on the women whose major interest in the trip was getting away from their husbands. Believe it or not, I've hosted more than a few of those — enough, in fact, for an entirely separate book. As I roll up my sleeves and start clearing the table, I recall one such woman, Doreen, who attended my Normandy class several years earlier, with three of her friends. I taught her quite a lot about French cooking, and she seemed to be paying attention. But afterwards I heard from her friends that she returned home to cook the same four dinners that made up her repertoire before the trip. It's true Doreen and her husband dined out a lot — she was always the first to tell me about the new restaurants opening in town — so I thought maybe that was the explanation.

Anyway, a few years later Doreen called me to say that she and her friend Nell wanted to attend my cooking classes in Tuscany. "Great," I said, "I'd love to have you!" I'm always flattered when a former student books another tour with me — especially in Doreen's case, since nothing she learned in Normandy seemed to have stuck with her. I sent her the registration materials and waited, but after a few days I hadn't received any confirmation.

Finally I phoned her and asked her point blank: what's up?

"I can't go to Tuscany with you and Nell," she admitted meekly.

"Why not?" I asked, surprised.

"It's Chuck," she said. Her husband. "He says I never cooked anything from the last time I spent with you, so he won't shell out good money to send me again." Well... this was disappointing, but clearly it was her own fault. All she had to do was make her husband a few new meals now and then to show him what he'd paid for. She blew it.

It was ironic. She'd only signed up to get away from her husband... and now she was stuck with the guy. I make a mental note to tell Doreen's story to Mary. Cooking might not be her main reason for the trip, but she'll be spending a week with a certified chef in a renowned culinary capital and she'd be well advised to bring something home to show for it, or next time she might find herself grounded.

The following day, two of Madge's out-of-town friends come through with confirmations... and checks. I've now filled every available opening in the class. Summer in Tuscany is *on*.

8
otto

The History of Castello Di Uzzano

THE RENTAL HOUSE I OCCUPY SIX MONTHS OF THE YEAR sits on land that was once part of the hill property of Castello di Uzzano. The villa was originally built in 1228 and sold in 1644 to the Masetti family — at the time, the third largest banking family in Italy (the first being the Medici, who retain that honor to this day).

It was once a vast tract of a hundred hectares (approximately 250 acres) consisting of stables, a church, a rectory, and small homes for the workers of the estate, as well as vineyards and gardens of historic repute. Subsequently the properties were subdivided and sold to locals, who renovated the property and began renting the smaller buildings and apartments to tourists like me.

The main villa has recently been acquired by the famous Louis Vuitton family, owners of the most popular leather brand in the world. "To think we live on the same street," I'll say to them whenever we run into each other at the local butcher shop.

I've often wondered for what reasons my particular house had been sold, along with the other properties over the years, and indeed why its vast grounds have been sold off. I inquire of the locals, "What's the story?" Surely my landlord ought to know, seeing how he's the owner of an original piece of Masetti property.

He does know. And over a glass of rich, warm Chianti, and a pasta dinner he tells me the story. It goes like this:

After the Masetti family acquired the villa, it remained their home for hundreds of years. Meanwhile, the once-large family declined. Finally the property passed into the hands of the sole remaining heir, who was single and childless. Late in his life, this Count Masetti unexpectedly married a Swedish blonde bombshell. "Possibly you will recall the headlines," my landlord tells me. "This is not so long ago, just a few years. Recent history."

The new Countess, seeing that the property was in desperate need of repair, undertook the restoration of several of the outbuildings. She apparently had no reservations about spending her husband's money, and the locals likewise had no reservations about taking it from her. In fact, they grew positively greedy, overcharging her astronomically. When the roofer completed his labor, the time he spent should have valued at 10,000 lire. He presented instead a bill for 100,000. "And everyone else shamelessly followed suit," my landlord continues, pouring more Chianti into his nearly empty glass. "The plumber, the electrician, the stone mason... the list goes on. And the Contessa, she just paid, you know? There were perhaps ten, twenty buildings on the property that she was trying to save, so she was paying hundreds of thousands of lire, no questions asked.

"Apart from the restoration," he continues, "she had a passion for breeding thoroughbred racehorses, and she indulged it without caution. She would travel to northern Africa, to the best breeding farms she could find, and purchase stock for her own stables. Money was no object. I am unaware of her other appetites, I never met her and know of no one who is acquainted with her, but she must have had many other desires for fine things, enough to drain a nobleman's inheritance like water from a sink."

Which is eventually what happened. Whether the Countess depleted her husband's bank accounts deliberately or ignorantly, we can never know; but we do know how she reacted once she'd wrung him dry. She said something to the effect of "Seeya 'round, bucko, I'm outta here," and left him high and dry.

The Count, who being old-aged had perhaps been too dazzled by his wife's beauty to see what she was doing to him (or too smitten to tell her to stop) was now left worse off than ever: he was alone, and a pauper. He had nothing left but the property, which he began selling off bit by bit, piece by piece. A house here, a parcel of land there, until all of it — from the buildings to the vineyards — were gone. He kept only the villa itself, its contents, and its immediate grounds.

"And to think," my landlord says, shaking his head, "that such a man was forced in the autumn of his life to give up his patrimony and live like a commoner. He had of course never held a job, and was now too old to begin. So there was nothing else he could do but what he did. Yet it must have been a bitter pill to swallow."

Eventually the Count was forced to let go of the villa's grounds, and then its furnishings as well. Christie's, the famous action house, conducted the sale. The locals, as well as many others, were very curious about these fabled contents. The villa's gardens had been world renowned and welcomed many visitors over the years but virtually no one had seen the inside of the villa. The Masettis, like most nobility, consented to mix only with their own class and there were very few such people left as the 20th century drew to a close. The only time a Masetti ever consorted with someone from a different class was when the Count married his Swedish wife, and given how badly that turned out it was unlikely to persuade any other nobles to be more democratic.

On the day of the viewing arranged by Christie's, people showed up to see, for the first time, the exceptional acquisitions that filled the villa. Marble statuary of various sizes and magnificence filled the halls; tapestries and ancestral portraits cloaked the walls. It was all exquisite, and by the end of the sale, it was all gone. The chandeliers from the ceiling came down, the rugs were sold in lots. Priceless porcelain went to the highest bidder, chairs were sold in pairs and tables in sets. Centuries' worth of collectibles were broken up and dispersed. "History itself was dismembered in this terrible affair," my landlord concludes, "lost forever."

And then, inevitably, came the sale of the house itself. Few villas of this size are available in this part of the world; and beyond that, it's a majestic edifice to behold, flanked by commanding staircases on the exterior and the internationally acclaimed gardens in the rear. It's grandly positioned at the top of a hill looking down on the town of Greve, with commanding views of the fabled hills of Tuscany.

My landlord has grown too sad and reflective — aided, perhaps, by the Chianti — to answer many more questions. So alas, I don't know how exactly the villa was sold — by real estate brokers, perhaps, or again at auction. What I do know is that it was sold to Louis Vuitton for a remarkable 14 million euros — with the cost of the renovations promising to be on par with that of the house itself. Then there's the furnishing of the interior to consider. Certainly the Vuitton family are possessed of very fine taste, so who knows just how many millions it will take to dress those many, massive rooms in a style that suits them? I for one will never know, for I don't travel in those lofty circles and am unlikely ever to step foot across the threshold.

Despite the many downward turns in my story of Castello di Uzzano, it ends on a surprisingly upbeat note. It seems the Count's errant wife has returned to him, and that they are actually now living together happily in the village of Greve. For her to burn through all of his money and hurl him into bankruptcy, then return to him in his declining years — and be forgiven and accepted by him! — it must be true love. Although a cynic might say, "Of course she came back, he's rich again." After all, with the proceeds from his liquidation there must be more than sufficient funds to secure him till his life's end. And there's no heir to the estate to squabble with him over it. Remember, the sale of the property alone was 14 million; but of course who knows how much debt there was in the end?

The villa has been under renovation for the last four years. I'm not sure when it will be finished, but I think things must be wrapping up. Four years ago, when the work began, a convoy of trucks, cars, and motorcycles could be seen heading up the hill beginning at about eight each morning, and not abating for half and hour. Now the morning flow to the villa has become much sparser. Yet there is still construction being done on the site, and other projects being completed. I've seen the transformation of the villa from sleepy giant to regal grand dame on the Tuscan landscape.

Meantime, I wish you luck in your new life, Count Masetti. May you prosper and live out your days with splendor, grandeur, and rejuvenation. God bless.

nove

The Luggage My Students Lug With Them

I AM NO LONGER TAKEN BY SURPRISE by the sheer volume of luggage my students show up with they arrive for a Culinary Vacation. From start to finish they'll be with me just five nights and six days, but to look at some of them you'd think they were settling in for a six-month tour of duty.

I know that most women like to shop. If a group has been in Florence a few days before I meet them, well, yes, I can certainly understand why they're carrying twice their own body weight in luggage. I can respect that they've spent no small amount of change on gifts to bring back as reminders of their trip, not to mention gifts for family and friends. It's quite understandable. I do the same thing, straining my shoulder by lugging home quantities of such irresistible items as dried porcini mushrooms in bulk, affordable half-gallon bottles of Grand Marnier liqueur, which I use for cooking, bars of my favorite olive-oil soap or a few dozen very large 18th century linen napkins that I can't find in the States. These are the kind of treasures I personally seek out when shopping in quaint little villages in Italy: unique finds unavailable (or else much more expensive) in the States. I've taken many a student to buy another suitcase for the additional purchases they've acquired while on vacation with me for a week.

And yet — there are travelers whose luggage is *already* monstrous when they arrive, before they've even had a chance to shop. They seem to come in several varieties. There's the kind who carries just one suitcase, but that one suitcase is stuffed to its limit, bulging at the sides in a way that threatens to burst at any moment, possibly with lethal consequences to those standing closest to it. Then there are the heavy travelers who arrive with a fully-packed medium-sized bag and mysteriously leave with several more bags, as though their original suitcase has given birth to a litter during their stay. And then there's the kind best represented by a Midwestern couple who met me in Florence, gasping for breath and shiny with sweat, having somehow made it this far with two virtually unliftable suitcases as well as a carryon for each of them. I almost popped a blood vessel getting their bags into the van. I'd have sworn they were filled with slabs of concrete.

It's true couples usually bring the most and largest bags. Maybe they have to dress up for each other. But we're a cooking school; dress here is on the casual side, at least in class. Some students do like to spruce up a bit when we take our tours, or go out to dinner, or when I invite a local friend to dinner. But those are just a handful of occasions; one or two special outfits would be plenty to cover them. I have no idea why these people insist on packing so much, especially those whose trips begin and end at my school, with no further traveling. I watch these people eagerly, expecting a dramatic costume change every few hours.

And sometimes I get it. The prize fashion plate to date was a single fellow named Bob. That's right, a man. Usually men travel light, right? They don't need separate cases for makeup or jewelry or hats, or a variety of shoes and handbags in matching hues, or a full spectrum of eyeglass cases. Most men can get by with just two pairs of shoes and a belt to go with each. A reversible belt would be even better. In fact the majority of men who come to me bring just a few days' worth of casual clothes for class and maybe a jacket and slacks to don for excursions.

But Bob was different. He arrived with two mammoth valises — just short of steamer trunks. The zippers on each were almost audibly groaning with the pressure against them. As if that weren't enough, he also had a backpack and a carryon— and the carryon was jumbo-sized as well. I was amazed they'd allowed it on the plane. He could've transported a decent sized dog in that thing.

"Wow," I said with awe in my voice. "What exactly do you have in there?"

He blushed and said, "Oh, this and that."

Thinking he was going to be a light traveler (single guy, remember?), I'd put him in his own bedroom on the third floor. I usually help my guests with their bags, so I went to grab one of Bob's valises, thinking, *This isn't going to be pretty; maybe I can pretend it's a gym workout.* But Bob surprised me by saying, "Oh, don't bother, I'll take care of these myself." I looked at him like he was crazy — not only should he have been glad of my help, he could've used a small crew of Egyptian slaves to get those monsters up three flights of stairs. But he insisted that I leave it to him. I think, on reflection, he was embarrassed about how much the bags weighed, and didn't want to see me grunting and groaning on his account.

Still, I had to wonder what he had in all that luggage. In fact we all wanted to know. The only certainty was that whatever it was, he'd brought it with him from the States. He'd only just arrived in Europe, and this was his first stop, so he hadn't had time to do any shopping before meeting us in Florence. He was, however, staying on after our Culinary Vacations week. I'd agreed to accompany him and another student to Rome for a few days, and show them around before heading back to Atlanta where we all live.

As the week unfolded, we all learned precisely what was in those very large valises from the States: clothes. Clothes, clothes, and *more* clothes. Bob changed outfits every time he had the opportunity. Each day in class he would appear in a different chef's outfit. Possibly you've seen them on TV right: those flashy slacks in a variety of crazy, colorful fabrics. Or it might be a denim chef's jacket to accompany the denim-colored vegetables adorning his pants. Or a black chef's coat to accompany the black pants festooned with bright red chili peppers. Always a well-coordinated uniform, with a pair of black chef's clogs. Sometimes when he felt the urge, he'd literally top it off with a tall white chef's toque.

After class Bob would change into something new for our excursions. And when we got back, he'd change again for dinner. After a week, we still hadn't seen him in the same ensemble twice. And when he and I moved on to Rome, I was amazed that he was able to produce even more clothes that I had never seen him wear before. It must've been an exhausting task, hauling it all around. I wonder who he was trying to impress?... Well, he impressed me, certainly, but probably not exactly the way he intended.

I myself pack for six days, and only six. That's how many days I'm with students. If you stayed with me for a month you'd see the same six days' worth. They're my cooking school clothes. When I look at photographs of myself with my students and I'm wearing my long-sleeve denim shirt, then I know it must have been a Sunday. I always wear my blue denim shirt on Sundays.

I don't wear a chef's jacket in Europe; it's too hard to keep clean when there is no dryer. So I just wear casual slacks, and shirts that have my logo on them. Keep it simple. Each group sees the same clothes.

That said, I have to admit I tend to arrive in Tuscany with a lot of luggage myself. But then I'm always bringing more items for the school: more kitchen towels, printed aprons, a few more wooden spoons, new tablecloths, a few more cloth napkins, and so on. Sometimes I'll pack food items as well. For instance, I can't find good powdered sugar in Italy, so I bring it with me from the States. Ditto with nuts, which are ridiculously expensive in Europe. I'll also bring domestic brands of baking powder and baking soda, because I want the measurements I give my students to work exactly right when they get home, and the products in Italy just aren't the same. And what about measuring cups and spoons?... We're not on the metric system, so they have to come over from the States as well.

As I've noted, when I return home the reverse is true. After I've emptied my luggage of the American goods, I can refill it with things I can't get (or can't afford) in the States. Lavender and truffle honey, Pecorino and Parmesan cheeses, amaretto liquor, European wines with fewer sulfites. Add in sugar for making my preserves, which already include the pectin. Vanilla beans as large as my fingers and *cheap*, I'm tellin' ya. Pink salt from the Himalayas, fleur de sel from Provence. Lemon verbena soap... well, the list goes on. So you see I can understand why luggage gets heavy.

It's when *they* arrive with that much luggage that I don't understand it. But I suppose that's human nature.

10

dieci

Porchetta Oggi

BY NOW IT SHOULD BE CLEAR that a Culinary Vacations week isn't spent entirely in the kitchen. I also conduct the students on a number of different outings. We visit vineyards, a pottery factory, a leather manufacturer (Italian leather is world famous), and of course shop for groceries. But we reserve Thursdays for venturing out to the small villages that dot the landscape of the Tuscany countryside. We call it "Village Exploration Day." What it really means is that everyone finally have a chance to S. H. O. P.

After so much intensive cooking, students are eager for the chance to relax and pick up a variety of items to bring home for the family or loved ones. There are innumerable shops offering everything from racy Italian magazines to fine *objets d'art*, so there's much excited chatter as we cross the center of any given certain town. But on this particular occasion, I'm the one who comes to an ecstatic halt when I notice the sign hanging outside the local butcher shop: *Porchetta Oggi* — "porchetta today."

Behind me, one of my students, a woman named Anna, has her eye on a shop window filled with scarves and blouses — and the shop-keeper in the doorway has her eye on Anna. "Um, Chef John... ?" she asks, her fingers already twitching around the clasp of her designer handbag. She's clearly a woman on a mission.

"Feel free to do your own thing," I say, releasing her from my authority "but anyone who wants a genuine Tuscan experience should come with me." Anna scampers off, driven by her shopping demon, but several others, intrigued by the excitement in my voice — and the light in my eye — follow me to the butcher.

Porchetta oggi. In most of the better or larger butcher shops, they still take the time to prepare this culinary Tuscan trademark. The butcher starts out with a whole pig — good hardy pork of the kind the Tuscans are known. No delicate seafood here. The entire animal is deboned with the head left attached. It's then place on a large flat surface and filled with a combination of fresh rosemary and thyme, a good sprinkling of salt and pepper, and a generous dose of chopped garlic, so generous that its aroma will exude from your pores after you've eaten. The pig is then rolled up, trussed, and roasted at a low temperature for as long as two days. Then it's allowed to cool and, finally, it's presented on a slab in the butcher shop and sold by the weight. You can ask for as much or as little as you like.

You'll also find porchetta at the counters of most pork venders at the open-air markets in the center of town. The pig's mouth is usually filled with an apple, at is the custom most of the year. At Christmas you may well find it wearing a crimson stocking. In the market porchetta is usually sold with a roll, or the vendor himself makes sandwiches out of it. So you can eat it while strolling around, shopping for other provisions. (While you're at it, I recommend you buy the fries as well.)

I first tasted porchetta several years ago. Several students had arrived a day early, so I said, "Let's go to the market in Pazano, I'd love for you to see this wonderful little village." We spent some time wandering through the colorful, aromatic market, after which I suggested we see what the butcher had to offer for lunch. "We can take it back to the villa," I said. "That way I can have a bite to eat before I have to head off to Florence to pick up the other students."

And so we entered Cecchini, the famous butcher shop where Signore Dario presides over the meat counter like a king over a royal court. It seems whenever you arrive at the shop, there's always a party going on. On entering you're handed a glass of Chianti and asked to sample the wares from a buffet table. One of the offerings is whipped fat served on bread. (I now caution my students about that one.) Anyway, on this occasion we bought a large slice of porchetta and several other delicacies, and picnicked on the grounds of the villa. Believe me, it wasn't easy to tear myself away from that feast and climb into the van for a long and lonely drive to Florence. Were I a lesser man, those arriving students might have found themselves stranded at the railway station.

Porchetta is usually eaten at room temperature. When I see it out on the slab at the butcher, I wonder how long it takes to sell the whole pig. Certainly not nearly as long as it takes to make it, and undoubtedly not long enough to raise any health concerns. That's the reason for the sign out front: the butcher who says "porchetta today," is implying "but maybe not tomorrow."

Since we can't all reproduce this Tuscan classic, I've created a home version I call *Porchetta Finta*, or "Pretend Porchetta". I simply use a pork loin instead of the whole pig. The filling remains the same and it's still slow-roasted for several hours. Whenever I bite into my *porchetta finta* I recall the Tuscan butcher's prize, because the taste and texture are very similar to the original. Enjoy!

PORCHETTA FINTA

1-4 lb boneless pork loin	8 garlic-cloves-minced
3 Tbs. fresh rosemary-minced	salt and pepper
2 Tbs. fresh thyme-minced	1 lb. bacon

Butterfly the pork loin and evenly pound it to about ½ an inch all over.

Evenly spread the rosemary, thyme and garlic over the loin and season heavily with salt and pepper.

Roll up the pork loin and wrap the bacon strips around the loin covering the entire loin. Tie with butchers twine at about ½ inch intervals.

Place in a shallow pan and bake in a 350 oven for about 2 to 2 ½ hours.

For a more tender, falling apart, porchetta, roast for the full 2 ½ hours.

Remove the twine and slice in ½ inch pieces to serve.

undici

Teaching The World To Play Pick or Push

WHEN I WAS GROWING UP, card games were one of my family's favorite activities. Especially for my mother; I think she got the bug from her own family — though not in the way you might think. My grandfather was a minister who preached against playing cards on Sunday. I'm not sure where in Scripture he got that. It could have been his own personal rule. Anyway, for my mother, it was a case of a forbidden fruit seeming much more appetizing.

Just a few years ago my mother asked her cousin if they ever played cards on Sunday, and she said, "Why yes, what else is there to do on Sunday?" So now Mom sees it as a proper activity, and there's no stopping her. In fact I think she's trying to make up for lost time.

As a child I remember we played a lot of cards, especially during summers at our mountain home near Asheville, North Carolina. There were always a lot of hours to fill, up where the TV reception was somewhere between intermittent and nonexistent. Over the years we ran through the whole repertoire of classics: hearts, rummy, canasta, even a little poker — but never Bridge. We just weren't a Bridge family.

Some people, I've found, don't "get" card games. Its like pulling teeth to convince them to play, and they don't enjoy it when they do. I've learned that this is something you leave alone. You don't force anyone to take part in an activity against their will. Their ill humor can end up ruining it for everyone else.

As I mentioned in an earlier chapter, during a Culinary Vacations week we often have down time in the evenings, and I often fill those empty hours with games. And occasionally I'll put out feelers to see if anyone is interested in cards. And why not?... I like to be a good host and a reputable tour company, and that means keeping my students happy. If it makes me happy too, so much the better.

A popular card game at the villa is one which many people don't know, but it's been around for years. It's called Pick Or Push. When I was preparing this chapter I did some research in an attempt to find the exact rules. I even looked in Hoyle's Encyclopedia of Card Games. All to no avail. I couldn't even find a game that came anywhere close. So as a public service I hereby put forth a set of rules that are a slight variation from those I learned from mother:

Pick Or Push and its rules

Between three and eight eager card players can participate. The game requires 2 decks of cards, including the Joker from each deck. Each player is dealt 11 cards, face down. The remaining cards are placed in a stack in the center of the table, with the top card turned right-side up on the side of the stack. The object of the game is to go out with no cards remaining in your hand. There are 5 hands to each game, and the person with the lowest score wins.

Each hand is slightly different to complete the game.

First hand: For each player to open he or she must have three sets of three-of-a-kind.

Second Hand: To open you must have a run of four in the same suit and a set of three-of-a-kind.

Third Hand: To open you must have a run of five and a set of three-of-a-kind.

Fourth Hand: Three sets of three-of-a-kind, just to mix things up a bit.

Fifth Hand: A run of 7 and a set of three-of-a-kind.

Deuces and Jokers are wild. Also, deuces can't be played as a 2, only as a wild card.

Wild cards can only be played one for every 3 cards or two for every 5 cards, 7 cards, etc.

Once each player opens you can you play on each other's set of cards. For instance: if I open with a set of Aces, a set of 3's and a set of 5's, and I also have two queens and a king, and another player has opened with queens and kings, I can play my cards on their cards, thus getting rid of mine. For this reason, once everyone has opened you can go out pretty quickly.

During the game if you are open after your first hand, and it's the hand that you open with sets of three of a kind, you can play a run but it must be a run of four cards or more in the same suit.

So it's your turn and we begin the game. First you must decide what you want to do with the card that's face-up in the center. You either pick it up for yourself, or top it with a card facing down and push it to the person on your left (game play proceeds clockwise). If you have pushed the cards to your left, then you get to take a card from the top of the pile. And when you are through with your turn, you must discard. To end the game and go out, you must have a card to discard or you don't win.

Okay, that's basically it. If I've left something out, I apologize — make your own rules to cover it. It's that kind of game. My mother's cousin, for instance, has her own variation on these rules. It's all good. Just carry on and have some fun.

I have to confess, sometimes it's hard to find a group of four people to play in my group of eight students. Once I had a couple who initially condescended to play, though without any real enthusiasm. I got the impression they were only doing it to appease me. Then we played and the wife won. The next night the husband was all fired up to play another hand so that he had a chance to take victory away from his spouse, but the novelty was gone and no one else wanted to play again. He didn't take it very well. In fact, he sulked all through class the next day.

I'm proud of what I've accomplished with Culinary Vacations, and with the new skills, new ideas, and new worlds I've introduced to my students. But you know, I think my mother is probably proudest of all for she taught me to play Pick or Push and I in turn am teaching the world to play pick or Pick Or Push.

12

dodici

The Big Pecorino

AFTER STARTING CULINARY VACATIONS, I'm determined to teach my students all aspects of cooking while they are under my guidance. I insist that they learn everything they don't already know. If they don't perform a culinary operation just so, I ask them to do it again. And so on, every day, till they get it right. I feel that if they're, say, dicing an onion incorrectly, they'll return home and do it in front of their friends, and that will reflect badly on me. Since I'm growing my business, I want my students' kitchen skills to do just the opposite: be such a dazzling testament to my teaching abilities that all their friends will sign up for my tours as well. So I start out as a bit of a drill-sergeant.

Then I find myself hosting a new group in Tuscany. This group is wild, fractious, and impossible to control but despite all our clashes they teach me something valuable: that while learning kitchen skills is important, so are laughter, camaraderie, and enjoying the Tuscan countryside. After all, you can take classes in vegetable dicing at home.

The group is formed by a magazine publisher named Donna and her equally successful, Type-A girlfriends. All are in their late thirties, with the exception of one guest's daughter who has accompanied her. From the start, they aren't what I'm used to.

They are, for example, a very athletic group. Each and every morning they leap out of bed, pull on their workout gear, and head up the winding road adjacent to the property. Then they climb the hill as far as they can in the time allotted, before turning around and race-walking back. A number of them carry their cellular phones with them — and this is back before it became easy to get a roaming signal. So as I'm cooking breakfast, I can tell when my students are drawing near by all the sharp cries of *"Hello?... Hello?... Hello?... "*

When they return, they all settle down for a complete stretching routine on the patio, which provides a stunning panoramic view of the surrounding countryside. I can hear them grunting and groaning as I put the finishing touches on the morning meal.

My usual continental breakfast comprises fresh fruit, flavored yogurt, breakfast breads, juice and coffee, served buffet style on the dining room table. Simple fare, since we'll be cooking and enjoying a full lunch and then later a full dinner. But this group isn't having it. They've requested eggs every morning.

"It's protein," Donna says, "to power those workouts."

"Do you have any idea how expensive eggs are here?" I tell her. "Around $3.50 and you don't even get a dozen. Just ten."

She shrugs, supremely unconcerned. "Add the cost to our bill."

"That's fine, but I'm not a short-order cook, you know."

"I'm sure you'll do just fine," she says, and turns on her heel, leaving me to fume.

So I condescend to make hardboiled eggs for the girls to wolf down when they get back from their morning trots. Mind you I wouldn't mind the chance to get some fresh air and exercise as well, since I've been putting on weight, as I usually do during these trips. But someone has to get breakfast on the table. (On the weekends, when I'm alone, I'm free to hike up the hill whenever I like. But when I do, inevitably some Italian friend will pull up beside me and ask if I want a ride. They don't understand the American mania for exercise.)

The morning routine repeats in the evening, as I busy myself with the next day's prep work while the women do yoga on the patio in the cool Tuscan dusk. This doesn't do much for my mood — or my waistline. (In fact it's only when I return home and see photos from the trip that I realize just how much I've gained. Then I have to buckle down and lose *thirty pounds*. Thanks, gang. Next time *I* walk and *you* cook the damned eggs.)

There are other problems as well. Every one of the women seems to have a "food issue" — something she won't eat. Tanya is dead-set against any kind of oil, Marybeth lives in horror of salt, Gwen won't touch any food "that used to have a face." Sometimes, however, the issue is legitimate, as in the case of Karen, who is allergic to dairy and thus can't have any of the cheeses. Eventually I convert her to pecorino. "It's made from sheep's milk," I tell her, "so it's perfectly safe for you." So from that day forward, whenever we break out the cheeses, Karen calls out "Where's my pecorino?"

Finally, the ice breaks. It's laundry day. As I'd warned everyone in advance, there's a washer but no dryer. With utilities costing triple what they do in the States, a dryer is a luxury item for Europeans. Here, you hang your laundry out to dry in the Tuscan sun. On clear days you can see clotheslines everywhere sagging beneath the weight of just-washed laundry. It's one of those sights that brings home just how spoiled we Americans are; we just don't know it till we spend time in a foreign country.

So I'm outside under the trees setting the table for dinner — getting things ready well in advance, which is my preferred way of doing things. Just as I'm finishing up the place settings, Donna sprints up the driveway — the last bit of her afternoon run. As she catches her breath, she sees the day's laundry drying on the rack outside the house. She reaches over and with two fingers delicately picks up what appears to be a very small pair of green thong panties.

"Whose are these, I wonder?" she asks in great curiosity with a huge grin on her face.

With a completely straight face, I tell her, "They're mine." And I resume my work.

She laughs. "As if you'd ever squeeze your ass into these!"

I look slyly up at her. "You'd be surprised."

"I'd be *astonished*."

"You want to see?"

A glimmer of doubt flashes across her face. "Are you serious?"

I walk over to her and extend my hand to take them from her. "You don't believe they're mine? I'll prove it. Just say the word, I'll put them on."

"All right," she says, calling my bluff. "Deal."

I reach out my hand to take them and at that moment, from a window above us, Marybeth shouts out, *"What are you two doing with my underwear?"*

Donna and I collapse into laughter. Between howls, she says, "I can't believe — I actually thought — for one *second* —" Marybeth, looking down on us, can't imagine what we're laughing about, and we're too gripped by hysterics to tell her.

From then on, Donna and I share a friendly, teasing relationship that soon spreads to include the others. Amazingly, I find myself having more wine with them after dinner. I usually don't drink much with my students. I'm the group leader, right? In control and on the job? But one of the wonderful things about a Culinary Vacations tour is that it forms, for the duration of the week (and sometimes longer), a little family. I'm learning this and liking it.

On Thursday night, their last with me, we uncork the Chianti and have a grand old time, hanging out together and reliving the highlights of the week. For a group of lean, wiry women, these gals can really put away the wine.

During dinner the group presents me with an apron from one of the local wineries. Each person signed it in gold ink. I'm very touched, and dutifully try it on.

Ever since the green thong incident, the humor between the ladies and me had been no-holds-barred bawdy, so once the apron is in place I stick my hand beneath it and poke it out at crotch level. They all hoot, but when Karen calls out *"The big pecorino!"* they nearly convulse with laughter.

To this day, whenever any of those women contacts me, she calls me "The big pecorino."

As for the apron, it now hangs in my wine cellar — memento of a wonderful week and a lesson learned.

13
tredici

Summer And The Schoolteachers

SCHOOLTEACHERS AS A WHOLE ARE GREAT PEOPLE. I've never met a more open bunch of individuals. They're candid and forthcoming, treat other adults like adults, and genuinely like and respect each other. They also seem to like to talk quite a lot, possibly because that's what they do for a living. So when I give my pre-cooking lecture for a group of teachers, I have to keep it moving or risk innumerable questions and conversational side-trips. Even so, my thirty-minute lecture often turns into an hour or so. And we have much work to do.

For several years now I've been able to offer my European trips to teachers for SDU (skilled development unit) or PLU (progressive learning unit) credits, which makes it more appealing to them. One such group is made up of Atlantans and a few friends from other parts of the country, who want to spend time together. They've decided Europe is a pretty good place to gather for summer break.

Two of them have been named Teacher of the Year by their respective schools, and none of the others are exactly slouches. So you'd think all the gales of conversation would be very elevated in tone. In fact, I quickly find out school teachers will talk to you about anything, and I mean *anything*.

We learn, for instance, who in the group is having bowel problems, which I am reassured is not from my cuisine because it began before they left Atlanta. We also learn who's suffering "that time of the month," who else might in fact be menopausal, and quite a lot of similar discussion of body fluids and functions. They are utterly frank about it all.

"I think we should cut down on Barry's garlic intake, Chef," one of them tells me midweek. "It's been twenty minutes since he left the bathroom and I *still* can't bear to go in there." And in the background, Barry just cackles.

Maybe the kids they teach talk this way and they've just gotten used to it. I myself am not accustomed to such open discussions; but they don't make me feel uncomfortable, just constantly surprised.

Given that they're all schoolteachers and I'm a college professor, it's inevitable that we end up talking about our students. Every night the stories flow— with the emphasis on the hilariously awful over the best and brightest. Even so, it becomes very clear that these teachers are really after their charges' best interest. They'll advance a gifted student and hold back one who needs extra attention, not from any personal agenda, but for the good of the student in question.

As usual I want everyone to absorb what is presented to them during the week, whether it be the procedure for making olive oil or the way to make biscotti or focaccia bread. My goal is to send each one home with new knowledge and skills, making their time in the kitchen both easier and enjoyable. To that end, all during the week I teasingly tell the teachers that they'd better pay attention because you never know if what I'm saying will end up on the final exam. I can see that some of them don't know how to take this; they really think I might be serious. And in fact I could very well test them at the end of the week. But we're in Italy, and I don't want them worrying about a test when they can be observing the wonderful way of life here. I want them to pay attention to the world outside the classroom and immerse themselves in Tuscan culture and traditions. Being in Europe with me is a life experience, one whose value I always say surpasses the dollar amount spent on the trip.

One delightful teacher, Sheila, takes this to heart and becomes very enamored of Italy. She falls in love with its people, its breathtaking scenery, its history, *everything*. She's a single gal with a problematic boyfriend back home (remember, they talk about everything). As the week goes by, I witness Sheila shedding the need for her troubled relationship and beginning a new one, with *la bella Italia* — or rather, with the confident, life-embracing woman Italy shows her who she really is.

"I want to learn to speak a little Italian while I'm here," she tells me one day, after we've been listening to two women at a market converse in bright, musical tones for twenty minutes. And in fact this is something I always try to instill in my students. So I begin giving Sheila a few simple lessons on words and phrases she can use in nearly any situation.

One of the more difficult words to learn to use correctly is *prego*. Its literal translation is "I pray you," but it's used in a variety of situations. As you enter a store the shop owner might greet you with "Prego" and after you've thanked him for his service he'll say "Prego" again, much as we say "You're welcome" in the States. It can be used as an encouragement or an enticement. Many uses for one word, like a catch-all phrase. But nothing to do with spaghetti sauce from a jar, as it is in America.

Another word often misused in America is *marinara*. Italians say *ragu* instead, which again for us is a bottled tomato sauce. It's best, when coming to Italy, to forget any Italian you might have learned from a label.

Another word Sharon really likes, which is usually mispronounced by foreigners, is *grazie*, Italian for "Thank you." When you pronounce *grazie*, all the syllables are pronounced — *GRAHT-zee-ay*. The long A at the end tends to drop off when Americans use the word. This pronunciation means you're blessing God. A subtle but important difference. Even so, there are people who can't hear it; one student of mine never got it right all week long.

Sheila is so thrilled with these two words that she says when she has children she's naming them Prego and Grazie!

We spend some time learning other useful words. *Ciao*, for instance, means hello as well as goodbye, and once again every letter is pronounced. Americans are used to simply saying *chow*, but the way Tuscans say it, it rhymes with *meow*.

Aiuto is another helpful word — pronounced *ay-OO-toe*. It means, "help." If someone snatches your wallet on the street and runs away, *"Aiuto!"* is what you holler. But you don't use it to ask a salesperson to help you; then you simply use *Scusa* — *SCOO-za* — which means

"Excuse me."

I tell my students at the beginning of each week that we're all here to learn, and I mean *all*; not only will they learn from me, I'll learn from them as well. And as it happens, I ended up learning something from a schoolteacher named Michelle.

Michelle has spent some time in Florence before joining me, and when she shows up she's weighed down with purses she's bought on the streets. Everywhere in Florence you'll find illegal vendors pushing cheap knockoffs of expensive brand-name purses and wallets. I've seen these vendors plying their trade for years — they're in every major city where they can prey on tourist traffic — but I've never taken their bait because they boldly try to pass off their merchandise as genuine, and I'm insulted they think I'm that stupid.

However, as I look at Michelle's purses, I have to admit they do look pretty good. Also, Christmas is coming, and in a weak moment I did promise my sisters to bring them back some fabulous designer items from my European travels. And when Michelle tells me the pittance she paid, my resistance dissolves. I ask her for a lesson in judging the quality of the bags, and on negotiating a sale.

She proceeds to show me details of the construction, stitching and so on, that I should look for if I want something approaching the quality of the real thing. She also tells me how much she was asked for the bags, and how she whittled it down to what she finally paid.

So I'm ready. At the end of the week, I drop the teachers at the Florence train station, say my goodbyes, and then search for a parking space. I'm determined to make my first knockoff purchases. I stalk the streets of Florence in search of the ubiquitous street vendors. I only have a short time before I have to go and buy groceries for my next group.

I don't see any vendors. It seems that whenever I've been here before, I've been tripping over them, and now that I actually want them they're maddeningly elusive. Maybe the police are cracking down on them, and now they only dare come out after dark. I walk and I walk, combing the back streets, the side streets... the Piazza del Duomo and the Ponte Vecchio. No street vendors. I double back and search the streets again. Not even a glimpse. What am I going to do? I've promised my sisters. I'm armed with a wad of cash for the big sale, and I am desperate to buy those purses.

Finally I spot someone who by his furtive manner looks like he may be selling the kind of contraband I seek. I tail him to see what he's going to do. He motions me to walk with him to a side street. There he unfolds a rather ratty blanket to show me his collection of purses. I see two or three that I want to buy. He tells me the price. It's much higher than the asking price Michelle got. Possibly I've let my eagerness show. (Possibly? *I am clutching money in my hand.*) I try to pull back, act casual, but it's too late; clearly he has my number.

"You're crazy," I tell him. "These aren't the genuine article, they're knockoffs. I'm not paying that kind of money for fakes."

He shakes his head. "No, no, signore, these are the real thing, that's why my prices are higher than the others. I don't sell no fakes. I'm an honest businessman."

I don't believe him, of course but it's too late for me to find another vendor. I make a counter offer. He comes back with a slightly lower price, which still would mean giving him all my cash. I tell him so. "If I paid you that, I wouldn't have money left to get my car out of the garage."

He smiles, obviously knowing he has me cornered. "How much does it charge, this garage?" he asks. I tell him, and he generously deducts that much from his price. Embarrassed and out of time, I take the purses and go.

I've just been ripped off. I was desperate and I let it show, like an idiot. But what's done is done. I made up my mind that I had to have these purses, and now I have them. And my sisters will love them. They do look real, and they're packed in nice cloth bags, just like they use in the real Louis Vuitton store. But I paid way too much. Next time, I'll be armed with guts and determination. And I'll allow more time.

Sure enough, the next year I go back to try my luck again. This time I'm staying in Florence for a few days before my school starts, so I'm not rushed. I go out into the streets after dark and the vendors are everywhere — so much so that the competition is good. As I stroll by, seeming uninterested, each vendor offers me a lower price, trying to attract me away from his rival. They're selling bags for next to nothing. I can't imagine how they make any profit at all.

The vendors keep hounding me, it's their technique. They come at you till you buy something. Finally, I see a purse I like. I shop many vendors to get the best price. Twenty dollars. What a deal! It beats the $150 I spent the year before. I close the deal and think, *Now I'm even*. No more shopping for knockoffs. My sisters have enough and besides, they say that they don't last; theirs have already fallen apart. I tell them to take them to the Louis Vuitton store and have them fixed. "With what I paid for those bags," I say, "they should last forever."

Keeps them guessing, right?

I am not an advocate of buying these knock offs. Now there is a fine for people buying and supporting these "blanket vendors", so be aware.

quattordici

An Italian Christmas

YEARS AGO I READ AN ARTICLE in *Gourmet* about Florence at Christmas time. The story did a wonderful job of capturing the flavor and feel of an Italian city during the holidays. The accompanying photos were the icing on the cake — lots of colorful shots of the locals engaged in their traditional celebrations. I reread the piece many times, and made up my mind to someday experience an Italian Christmas myself.

Now I find myself doing just that — standing in a Tuscan hill town as snow brilliantly whirls around me. Yes, there's snow here, but rarely any real accumulation, just a light dusting.

It's my first Christmas in Italy and I've come here on my own. I'm testing new recipes and inviting friends from the surrounding area, most of whom aren't Italians but rather transplants from all over Europe and America.

It's exhilarating to be here. The decorations are joyous yet subtle, much in keeping with the simple, elegant European style. Garlands of fresh bay leaves hang high above the archway in the grocery store arcade, tethered with plain brown raffia. Large, unadorned fresh pine trees dot the parking lots and shopping areas of the small specialty shops in the village. Christmas lights do hang high above the city streets very much like in America, but without the sense of spectacle we have in the States.

The season is savored here, not rushed. Stores aren't laden with holiday merchandise well before Halloween. The yuletide begins to show its face in early November – "like a rabbit peeking out of a hole," as my friend Andrew puts it – just about the time we all turn our thoughts to what gifts we might choose for our friends and family.

Tradition is important in every country, and I like to understand and experience this wherever I am. And since I want to treat my expatriate guests to a traditional Italian Christmas dinner, I ask my Italian friends what I should serve.

My good friend Albarosa is insistent on one item in particular: "You must give them a *panetonne*." My heart sinks a little. I've seen these items in bakery shops — they're fruit cakes. The American holiday cliché.

But in fact a *panetonne* is unlike any American fruit cake, which usually range from bad to inedible. (Although a good American fruit cake can be great served with a dessert wine and some fine cheeses.) *Panetonne* may look similar — 6 to 8 inches tall, choked with dried fruits (a scattered garnish as I like to call it) and sold in a box, but *panetonne* is much lighter than its distant American cousin.

"The tradition is," Albarosa explains, "that you give to each of your friends a *panetonne* at this time of year." She sees my eyes grow wide as I calculate how many that could end up being. "Yes, it is a lot," she says with a nod. "But of course you too will receive that many in return!"

At the grocery later, people's carts are filled with only one item: *panetonne*. There are different varieties to choose from as well. But for the most part, I think they're all pretty tasty.

After the holiday Albarosa, who has many friends, calls to say, "I've never received so many *panetonne* before. I am surrounded by them! Can you think of anything I might do with them?"

"I'll show you how to turn them into bread pudding," I offer. "That'll be one way to put them to use. Even better, you can give the pudding to the same people who gave you the *panetonne*!"

PANETTONE BREAD PUDDING

4 large eggs	¼ tsp freshly grated nutmeg
2 cups whole milk	1-2 lb panettone-cut into ½" cubes
1 cup heavy cream	powdered sugar for dusting
1 tsp pure vanilla	zabaglione sauce
¼ tsp cinnamon	

In a large bowl, whisk the eggs with the milk, cream, vanilla, cinnamon and nutmeg.

Add the panettone and stir to coat. Allow to soak about one hour. Preheat the oven to 350.

Pour the batter into a greased 9x13 glass baking dish and push down for even baking.

Bake for about 40 minutes until puffed and golden. Remove from the oven and dust with sugar. Cut into squares and serve with the warm zabaglione sauce.

ZABAGLIONE

12 egg yolks	6oz sugar	6oz sweet Marsala wine

In a large metal bowl add the above ingredients and beat with a balloon whisk to dissolve the sugar.

Add the bowl to the top of a double boiler and cook until thicken and fluffy, mixing with balloon whisk for about 10 minutes until thick and pale. Serve warm with the panettone bread pudding.

quindici

New Year's In Tuscany

IT'S COMING UP ON NEW YEAR'S and I'm heading to Tuscany to host a group for the holiday week. To avoid the rush of travelers I'm leaving on Christmas and arriving in Florence the following day. Since this means I'll have to endure a Christmas dinner cooked by the airline, I decide to have a really great meal in Florence on the 26th and just consider that my Christmas repast.

One of my students, Silvia, is also arriving early from Puerto Rico, and we've planned to hook up, since we're both staying at the same hotel. It'll be nice to spend some time bustling around the city in the wake of the holiday — bundling up and walking the streets amidst the decorations.

In our correspondence, I discover that Silvia and I are going to be on the same plane from Milan to Florence so we agree to try to meet even earlier, at the airport. My layover is for several hours, giving me plenty of time to connect with her.

When I have a long layover, I usually find a seat in the middle of a crowd, park myself there, and engage in some old-fashioned people-watching. Eavesdropping too, of course, when the occasion permits. I'm a writer and isn't that what we do?... Record and then transcribe the goings-on and gossip we find around us?

Sitting there, I strike up a conversation with a couple of Midwestern ladies, Honey and Dot. They've been on a whirlwind tour of Italy, and Florence is their last stop before heading back to the States.

"You look like you've enjoyed yourselves," I offer, noticing the bags of duty-free shopping each woman has arrayed around her.

"Not enough," says Honey with a tinge of desperation. "I've got kids heading to college so this may be the last trip I take for God knows how long. I want to wring Italy *dry*."

Since I'm familiar with Florence, I offer to help out, suggesting we all meet up for dinner one night. They're delighted to have at least one decision taken off their hands. I give them the name of one of my favorite restaurants and its location, and we agree to meet there on the 27th at eight o'clock.

We continue chatting. I tell them all about my business and that I'm on my way to Tuscany for a New Year's Eve with a group of students from around the world: a Canadian couple, another couple from Atlanta, two women from Puerto Rico and two ladies from Florida. They're avid listeners and ask for many details. Before I know it, we're hearing the announcement that the plane is ready to board. This comes as a surprise. I'd hoped to hook up with Silvia. But Honey's caustic humor (and Dot's witty asides) have kept me so entertained I haven't even had a chance to look for her.

As we head for the plane I tell the women about Silvia and they help me pinpoint her in the departure lounge, so I just have time to meet her before boarding. She's somewhat petite and very chic. She reiterates that she's looking forward to seeing Florence with me before her friend and fellow student arrives from Puerto Rico to join her.

We reconnect in the Florence airport's baggage claim area, where both of us discover that our luggage has gone missing. Nothing brings fellow travelers closer together than disaster.

"Something goes wrong with every trip," I tell her, trying to keep her spirits up as we trek to the lost-luggage counter. "Maybe it's better to have it happen right at the beginning so you can get it out of the way. You know what they say: bad dress rehearsal, great performance."

She grimaces. "If I don't get my bags, this performance won't have any costume changes."

We continue quipping in this manner as we fill out form after form regarding our loss. Fortunately, this is occurring prior to the

2006 restrictions on carryons, and I've got a travel kit with all my toiletries, so I don't have to replace any essentials. Silvia, however, declares she must make an emergency cosmetics stop before leaving the airport.

In addition, the Florence airport does, in fact, give us each an emergency kit, which they have on hand for such cases. It contains the usual items one needs to carry on a somewhat normal life. In its contents is an undershirt. I want both mine and Sylvia's, because we don't know exactly how long it'll be till we're reunited with our luggage.

The airport also gives us an allowance to spend on clothing, totaling about seventy-five American dollars. I'm sure how much we can buy with $75; we can probably skip Prada and Gucci, that's for sure. But it's right after Christmas so perhaps we'll find some sales where we can stretch our money.

And so we arrive at our hotel with only our carryon luggage. But we've bonded now, and this feels like an adventure. Our spirits are high. As soon as we've checked into our rooms we bundle up and head out. The weather is really ideal, cold and crisp, yet sunny and bright. Silva is interested in just casually strolling Florence with me, because she's promised to withhold sightseeing until her friend arrives in a few days. So off we go, in search of new clothes.

We arrive at the big department store, Coin, rather than the pricey boutiques, because I want my money to go as far as possible. Underwear, slacks, and a shirt are really all I need. I'm hoping my $75 will cover that. Alas, no Target stores hereabout!

I find the men's department, where a young sales assistant takes one look at me and flees. He's clearly not about to waste his time trying to fit someone as tall and broad as I am. I shrug and grab several pairs of pants on my own — all from different places on the rack because I don't know my size in centimeters. Then on into the fitting room.

When all is said and done I try on about fifty pairs of pants. And nothing fits. I'm just not a typical Italian body. The pants are either too short or too long — too tight in the front or too tight in the back — or the rise isn't low enough for me. Giving up, I decide I'll just keep wearing the pants I've got on, and try for better luck in the shirt de-

partment. But there's nothing there I can't live without, and the prices are much too high. In the end I decide on one shirt — something
neutral in color that will go with many things and many seasons.

Next, underwear. Fifty bucks for a pair of designer underwear!
What are they made of, ermine? Who on earth would buy these?... I
can't imagine. I hold up a pair, ostensibly sized Large, and they look
like something you might see on a fifteen-year-old Olympic diver. I
move to the XL with no better luck so I decide on a pair of XXL. I'm
6´2˝ and weigh about 180, so maybe that's about right. I bring it all
to the counter, hoping I've done the right thing.

Silvia and I return to the hotel. Still no luggage. Oh well, at least
we have our new clothes. In the room before dinner, I try on my new
underwear. I look like... a fifteen-year-old Olympic diver. On a really,
really bad day. Oh, well.

At night we step out for our one-day-late Christmas dinner. Silvia
has managed to put together a whole new outfit from her $75, and
it looks sensational. This is a mysterious skill some women possess.
"You look terrific," I tell her.

"You must be joking," she says, but her eyes gleam. She's pleased
by the compliment.

I have an acquaintance, Mario, who sings at a restaurant in down-
town Florence, and I suggest we venture forth to see if the place is
open.

Closed for the holidays, alas. But on our way there we've passed
another promising-looking restaurant on the same street, so we head
back to give it a closer look. We're both foodies, remember, and we
want a special meal to make up for our having had Christmas dinner
on an airplane.

We look in the window. It's too early — Florentines (like most
Europeans) dine very late — and the staff is still rushing about, doing
last-minute cleaning and preparing for the night's guests. We ask to
see a menu while we wait. One is presented and we read its contents
with delight. The wine list is very promising as well, with many ex-
cellent wines by the glass. So we agree to make this our spot. When
they finally open for business, we secure a table and wait for a really
exceptional meal. It turns out to be a real find — the food is creative
and the wines are a bargain. Silvia used to be an importer so she

knows her varietals.

After the meal we sit back, utterly contented. "Merry Christmas," I say.

Silvia daubs her mouth with her napkin and says, "Same to you." She pats her stomach. "If I had another bite, I'd burst. And I can't afford to ruin this outfit. It's half my existing wardrobe."

By now the locals are beginning to trickle in. "Funny," I say as I signal for the bill, "they're just arriving for an evening out, and we're ready to call it a night."

"Well, we've had a long and frustrating day," Silvia says. Suddenly, as if having been reminded of this, we're both extremely tired. We stagger back to the hotel.

The next day is brightened by a late Christmas miracle — the arrival of our luggage. We spend the morning picking out clothes to wear from what now seems like an extravagant number of outfits, and only have a small amount of time to spend together in the afternoon.

Since Silvia and I enjoy each other's company, I invite her to join me at my dinner with the women I met at the airport, Honey and Dot. "I remember them," she says; "they seemed fun." So she's in.

The restaurant at which we're to rendezvous is several blocks from our hotel, but in the opposite direction from the way we've been going the past two days. This is exciting; in Florence, taking a left turn instead of a right can lead you into what seems like an entirely new city.

Before we reach the restaurant, I'm distracted by the sound of a familiar, bugle-like laugh. I look up to see Honey and Dot approaching us. "Ciao!" Honey calls out merrily. She jerks a thumb behind her and says, "Our restaurant's closed. Any other bright ideas?"

"As a matter of fact, yes," I say, and I lead everyone to the spot where Mario's singing. It won't be a memorable meal like last night's, as the restaurant is designed to serve tourists who won't return a second time. But it will be tasty, and it'll have atmosphere.

We get a good table near the center of the room. Mario is already behind the microphone, crooning away. He nods his greeting as I enter, and when he finishes his set he joins us. We make introductions around the table.

Dot seems dazzled by him. "You were wonderful, Mario," she enthuses. "Where'd you learn to sing like that?"

Mario says, "It's nothing, I am inspired by the beauty I see around me," and he looks straight into Dot's eyes. She almost giggles.

For the rest of the evening Mario sings to our table. Not ideal, for we'd wanted to get acquainted. But Dot seems happy. We become the center of attention for the entire restaurant.

Next morning I leave Florence to open the house and make preparations for the coming week. Two days later I'm back in Florence again, to retrieve all my students — including Sylvia and her friend — at the St. Maria Novella train station.

As I load the van I discover that one lady, Theresa, has no luggage. "The airline lost it," she says glumly. "They have no idea where it is. Apparently it might've been sent anywhere."

I commiserate with her as she climbs in the van. "The same thing happened to me," I tell her. "It took them a day to find my bags, but I did get them back." From the next seat up Silvia looks over her shoulder and says, "Me too — same exact story."

Theresa looks reassured. "I just hate the idea that my luggage might have gone someplace nicer than I have," she jokes.

"My dear lady, you're in Tuscany," I tell her as I get behind the wheel. "So that isn't humanly possible."

Fortunately, Theresa does have her carryon, which she seems to have stocked pretty well. When we reach the house she relaxes and enjoys the first night, reasonably confident her bags will arrive the next day — or the day after, at the latest.

Except... they don't. She calls the lost-baggage number dutifully several times every day and they never have any better answer for her. Her bags are just gone. Other people in the group begin to lend her items of clothing. I jokingly offer a pair of thong underwear. She declines. She does get a nightshirt, socks and many tops from the group. I don't understand why she doesn't just go out and buy a few things. She wears the same pair of jeans every day for six consecutive days, which makes me feel a bit itchy. Well, it's her prerogative.

Finally at midweek she stops bothering to call the luggage number. "I'll get it back when I get back home," she says.

And she does. We later learn that there was a major luggage snafu involving European flights from JFK. The bags just piled up and the pile got bigger every day. There was no way of stopping or sorting through this huge mass of lost luggage in time to do its owners any good while they were abroad. So the actual processing of baggage came to a halt (mind-boggling!) and all the suitcases and trunks were just sent back to their place or origin.

So it was a good thing Theresa stopped obsessing about it and moved on — another lesson for me. Since then, I always travel with the printed recipes for my students in my carryon. Because I can run Culinary Vacations without a change of shirt or even underwear, but what on earth would I do without the recipes...?

16

sedici

My Train Ride Into Italy

BEFORE I ADD A NEW COOKING CAPITAL to my Culinary Vacations roster, I travel to the location I have in mind and research all of its attributes that will bear on this new phase of my business. After operating in Normandy for two years, I'm anxious to add another destination and Tuscany seems to be *the* new hot spot. Americans are swarming there, buying second homes there, and writing scads of books about what they've done there. So off to Tuscany I go — not knowing quite where I'll end up, but that's what these scouting missions are all about.

My friend Jan wants to accompany me and help me find the ideal location. I'm grateful to have her along. Soon I have our map charted, our itinerary set, and our hotel rooms booked. While in each city we'll seek out unique establishments of culinary interest for my students' excursions. When we find a place that looks promising, we'll arrange for a tour so we can see if it's up to my standards, and also to gauge the staff's proficiency in English. I require tour guides for my students have some fluency in English because I want them to be able to interact with them.

I also look for entertainment value. If something is apt to bore my students, I'd rather find that out sooner than later. And of course I take into account the distance from our home base. Is this too far for a day trip?... Tuscany is a deceptively big place and I don't want to exhaust my students by spending all day in the van. Finally, I try to find places that, taken together, offer some variety. I've come to realize that every excursion isn't for taste. Like they say, you can't please all of the people all of the time. But when possible, I like to focus on attractions that have a culinary slant.

Jan is scheduled to fly over to France after my Normandy cooking class wraps up and spend a week at my house there enjoying some R&R. She wants me to meet her in Paris, after which we can both take the train back to Carentan. Well, that's about five hours out of my day — not to mention $200 round trip. Jan's a big girl (in more ways than one) so I tell her, "Find your way to Normandy and I'll meet you here."

I'm confident she can figure this out. I've armed her with precise instructions on what to do once she arrives in Paris. I can understand her reticence. She's never been to Paris before and speaks no French whatsoever. But the woman has a Master's degree, for God's sake. And I'm not asking her to kayak down the Amazon to reach me. Paris is a highly cosmopolitan city.

So on Sunday morning I meet her at the *gare*, train station, in Carentan. From the moment I see her, I know she's had a rough go of it. She's aggravated and almost in tears, and keeps angrily shifting her carryon over her shoulder, as though it won't cooperate and stay where she wants.

"Nice trip?" I ask — I can't resist myself — and she glares at me before giving up and breaking into a smile.

This kind of thing seems to happen frequently — students arriving to meet me, battered by confusion and uncertainty, their faces streaked by tears — tears of joy at seeing me, I can only hope. I don't know why some people have such a terrible time going from Point A to Point B. I guess there's a travel gene, and some unlucky souls are born without it. They lose all their self-confidence when they're on the road, or surrounded by strange environs.

Jan relaxes in the van as she relates her many misadventures in Paris and on the train to Carentan. Interestingly, every disaster she's suffered is a result of her panicking and abandoning my instructions, but I decide not to point this out to her. I know a trip to one of my locations can involve many steps, and I always provide explicit instructions to get you through them. For me, each leg of a journey is one step closer to a goal — something I can check off my list, and feel real progress. But for some people, each leg is a new time-bomb set to go off who knows when. Whenever I ask Jan why she didn't just follow my instructions, she says something like, "The man didn't answer me" or "There was another sign before the one you said that confused me." You have to just shrug and give up.

Her anxieties finally evaporate when she gets to the house, unpacks, has a drink with me, and then plunges into bed for a good night's sleep.

Next morning it's Monday — market day in the town of Carentan. If you've never been to a market day in a small European town, you don't know what you've been missing. All the vendors set up shop early, offering many different things in many different manners. It's as much theater as shopping. The day starts at nine-ish and the market doesn't close till twelve-thirty or one o'clock.

The night before, we agree to leave the house at nine. The earlier you go, the better your chances of getting a parking space. In Europe parking is always at a premium.

I've been up for a while — showered, dressed, and breakfasted — and now I notice it's five minutes to nine and I haven't heard a peep from Jan. So I go to her room, rap gently on the door and call out, "Time to go to market — are you ready?"

Silence.

This time I knock harder. "Jan, it's almost nine, I'm on my way out the door to the market. Are you with me or not?" No reply. "It's an open-air market and a real circus. You really shouldn't cheat yourself."

A long pause, then a voice heavy with sleep calls out, "Go on without me. I'm sleepin' in."

I frown. I hate to see people waste their limited time in Europe. They can sleep at home. "Are you sure?"

"Mm. Wake me when y' get back 'n' we'll have lunch."

Lunch?... By then the bulk of the day will be gone. Oh well, she has just flown over and she did have an emotional time of it and I shouldn't rule out jet lag. And I'm sure she had a hectic week beforehand, arranging everything at her job so that she could safely leave it for a week. You have to wonder sometimes whether it's worth the bother of going on vacation, it seems to take more and more work to arrange everything for while you are away.

So off I go to the market on my own. I'm in search of some hearty local produce for the week ahead of cooking for my friend. I also want to pick up a few household items we need. And it's always fun to see if anything new has arrived — flowers for the house, a chicken, and so on.

It's a cloudless day, the sun is out in force. It's glorious weather. I weave my way through the crowd. People all around me are chattering like magpies. I try and eavesdrop, picking up words here and there for some French is Greek to me.

I pick up whatever catches my fancy — some awesome croissants from my favorite bread vendor, a variety of fresh fruits from the market's best produce vendor, a couple of small pots of fresh herbs we don't grow already in the garden, and a couple more food items to keep us stocked up for the week. It's the same market with the same people. I've learned to recognize faces, and mine in turn is now familiar. I'm a regular, and a good customer. I stay loyal and buy from the same stalls each week (unless, of course, there should be better produce at another).

The last thing I want to do before leaving is to purchase something at the area of the market that functions as a kind of food court. There vendors serve an irresistible range of hot food to go: pizzas, sandwiches, and — my favorite — wonderful hot grilled sausages, *saucissons*.

There are also rotisserie-cooked quail, chickens, and hens that are ready to take away around lunchtime. The fowl is place on spits, with quartered potatoes and vegetables arranged in a drip tray at the bottom of the rotisserie. So when the chickens are ready you can also get an order of wonderful hot, fat-soaked cut potatoes. What a sweet life! There's even Asian fare for sale — a wide range of stir fries, with rice and eggrolls.

Usually at French markets there's an enormous paella for sale. The pan is about forty inches across and six inches deep, and it's filled with bubbling, heavenly-smelling paella. Once it's cooked you can buy whatever portion size you want — they'll package it up to suit you. If you go early, when the vendors are just setting up, you can watch them put together the foods they'll be selling come lunchtime. A paella this size takes a long time to make, so they have to start the preparation quite early in the day. And you can stand by and watch them assemble lunch. As I said, there's a big element of theater here. And the show is always on, because making paella involves adding ingredients as you cook.

I have to confess, while I've enjoyed the show, I've never bought the paella at the market before. I'm always a little wary about the prepared foods I buy. (Though I have in fact bought the whole roasted chickens before. They can be a little salty.)

I get in line at the sausage vendor to place my order. (I call him the "sausage vendor," but he also sells grilled pork chops as well as French fries. Which I have only bought once, when my group was openly salivating over them.) These people know me well. Whenever I'm in Carentan, you can find me here each Monday around 12:30, always ordering six to eight sausages. I get them plain, tucked in a roll. I'll apply my own condiments when I get home. The rolls are from lengths of a fresh baguette, crispy and crunchy on the outside, soft on the inside, sometimes even still warm. Spoiled?... Yes, I am. So sue me.

Sausages in hand, I hike it back to the car. As I pull out of my parking space, there's someone already behind me waiting for it, no doubt overjoyed by his luck at having it open up for him.

On my way back to the house, I find myself hoping Jan is awake and anxiously awaiting my return with lunch. Surely she must be ravenous by now.

After parking the car, I enter a quiet house. I call out, "Jan, are you up?" No reply. I call out again: "Hellooo, Jan?" Nothing.

I go and stand outside her bedroom door, and use my most honey-coated voice to say, "Jan, honey, are you coming out for lunch?"

I hear a rustle of sheets, then a brief pause and, "Uhh, no. Too tired. Just wake me for dinner."

Dinner! I think to myself. What on earth am I supposed to do until *dinner*?

I say, "But I've got fresh, hot sausages from the market." I'm hoping this will tempt her. Jan likes to eat and loathes missing a good meal.

"Save 'em for dinner," she says drowsily.

I'm completely flummoxed. I've never seen this side of her. She's always the adventurer, the explorer. What's up with her?... Whatever it is, it's beyond my power to deal with, so like a good host I put the *saucissons* aside and instead make a lunch of some potato salad I'd made on Sunday and a glass of white wine. I set it all up outside under the sun, and read my book as I dine, enjoying the day. This is one thing Europe has taught me — take whatever's there, and make the most of it. It's the best lesson anyone can learn.

Fortunately, by dinnertime whatever had Jan in its grip is gone, and we're able to enjoy each other's company for the rest of the week. Jan's able to get her R&R, and I'm able to get a set of dishes I've had my eye on for several years. I finally decide to buy them once Jan sees them and gives me her approval. I already own fifteen sets of dishes, ranging in size from a hundred place settings down to a dozen, so I don't acquire any more these days without active encouragement. These particular dishes are beautiful things, though. They're adorned with currants and leaves. I hate floral patterns on dishes — or on anything else, for that matter.

At the end of the week we close up the house and make an early start for Paris on Saturday morning. We drop the rental car at the Gare de Lyon train station and hop the six o'clock train for Italy, which — after changing trains once in Milan — will get us into Florence about five o'clock that evening.

The train ride is wonderful. I've never traveled this far by train before, and the rhythm is very relaxing. There's none of the boredom or itchiness you'd expect from an eleven-hour journey. In fact it's endlessly interesting to watch the scenery roll by. I can't think of a better way to see the countryside, certainly not driving, which divides your attention.

It's a quiet ride with only several other passengers on in our carriage. No one's really saying much. We all seem to be lulled by the journey, happy in our own heads. Seeing the French Alps covered with snow is really a highlight for me. As a native of Florida, now living in Atlanta, I don't come across this wonderful sight very often.

In Milan we run to catch our connecting train to Florence but unfortunately we've somehow missed it.

"How did we manage that?" Jan asks.

I shrug. "Who knows? We're in Italy. Things like that just happen here."

Fortunately, this upset to our plans doesn't bother Jan. She just steps back and lets me take charge of things. I guess she only lets travel glitches panic her when she's on her own.

Since we've missed our train we'll have to catch the next one, which means exchanging our tickets. I work out where that takes place, get in line, and wait.

And wait.

And wait some more.

The line is moving with all the zip of a glacier. Also, word comes back to me from those ahead that the agent at the counter doesn't speak any English. So this is going to be one of those trials you have to get through when traveling. Well... better me than Jan.

After an hour, I reach the head of the line, where I'm told (in a hybrid of English and Italian that takes some figuring out) that in order to get on the next train we have to pay an additional 3,000 lire apiece for our ticket change. I try to explain that it was the train line's fault we were late and we therefore shouldn't have pay *anything* extra. But the ticket agent only looks at me blankly. I might as well be speaking Urdu.

I storm off in hopes of finding someone in authority who also speaks English. At last I find someone who tells me to go and stand in another very long line and take my complaint up with the people at that counter.

Another line, another pint-sized eternity. As I'm waiting I calculate how long each customer is taking at the window. I multiply this by the number of people ahead of me, trying to determine how long it'll be before I get my chance to make my complaint. A little mind stimulus to pass the time. Eventually I find myself next in line. I have my story ready and I'm sticking to my guns. 3,000 lire?... That's absurd.

Finally, hallelujah, I'm at the counter — a full seven minutes earlier than my calculation, which makes me feel even more energized.

I look the agent square in the eye and say, "All right, here it is. My friend and I just came from Paris, but our train arrived late so we missed our connecting train to Florence. So we have to exchange our tickets for the next one available. I've been told there's a charge of three thousand lire per ticket to make that happen, but since we missed our connection through no fault of our own, I can't see why we should have to pay anything extra. The airlines don't operate that way, you know."

The agent understands, fortunately, but doesn't appear able to make a decision. Instead he asks his supervisor to come over. I take a deep breath and explain the entire situation all over again.

"I understand, Signore Wilson," he says. "But you see, the train you wish to take to Florence will be serving a meal, and it is for this reason that the there is an extra charge."

To me, this is Alice In Wonderland logic. "What do I care about a meal?" I say. "Just don't serve it to us. We only want to get on the train."

"You may choose not to eat the meal, if you like," he says. "But there is no discount for doing so. The ticket price remains the same."

"I'm not asking for a discount," I say, feeling myself getting hot under the collar. "I'm asking you to honor the tickets I bought in good faith, that your own lateness prevented me from using."

It's useless. He looks at me with the hard, set eyes of someone who has been through this scene countless times without ever once breaking. "This I regret I cannot do," he says. "You may, if you wish, walk to Florence instead, for which choice I will be happy to give you a full refund."

What else can I do? I'm checkmated. It really is this next train, or walking. So I swallow my pride and shell out the extra six thousand lire for the two tickets.

As I'm walking away, fuming, I decide to calculate just how many dollars I've wasted, just to torture myself. As I do the conversion in my head, I realize to my shock and embarrassment that three thousand lire comes to just about $1.50. I've spent almost two hours making a huge fuss over having to part with three lousy bucks. As I rejoin Jan, who's been waiting patiently by a fountain, she takes one look at me and says, "What are you grinning at?"

"Nothing," I say. "I'm just an idiot." As I explain the dollar amount for the new tickets I have just purchased. We have a big laugh together. What a goof ball.

The train to Florence is filled with energy and excitement, much different from our train ride from Paris. New scenery, people drinking and laughing and having a great time. Several of them even speak English and we're able to converse with the locals. We also decide in favor of the meal service after all, and it's delicious — a real bargain for $1.50 per person.

Jan turns to me and says, "I think I'm going to like Italy!"

And of course she did. Everyone loves Italy, which is why I wanted to do business there in the first place. There's something about the Italian climate, culture, and character that brings out the best in people, their warmest and most generous sides, and that's a big part of what Culinary Vacations is all about.

Which brings us full circle, back to the beginning of this book and my early days as an American chef teaching American students how to cook in Italy. Thank you for taking this journey with me. I've enjoyed being your guide through these many memories almost as much as I enjoyed living them.

I have many more stories to tell, from my other Culinary Vacations destinations and perhaps someday I'll set them down for you as well. So in closing I say, not *addio*, but *arrivederci*!

recipes

RECIPES FROM THE REGION

Beans are a staple in Tuscany. So I have developed this recipe which has lots of flavor to go with the almost uneatable breads of Tuscany. It keeps for a long time in the fridge. Great to have on hand for when unexpected guests arrive. I also use it in the place of mayo on a sandwich with sliced tomatoes, fresh mozzarella and even a fresh leaf of basil from the garden, when it's in season.

TUSCAN WHITE BEAN SPREAD

½ lb. Great Northern beans-cooked until soft
4 garlic-cloves-peeled
¼ cup onion-coarsely chopped
1 Tbs. fresh oregano-minced

¼ cup sour cream
¼ cup olive oil
salt and pepper
sliced bread or crackers

In the bowl of the food processor add the cooked beans, garlic, onion and oregano and pulse to blend. Add the sour cream and process. With the motor running add the oil in a steady stream. Season to taste with salt and pepper. Chill before serving. Serve with sliced bread or crackers.

Years ago during one of the first few wine tours in Tuscany, during the wine tasting we were served wonderful homemade crackers along with this great cold tomato sauce. It has taken me years to create this cracker, which is similar to the ones we were served at the winery. The tomato sauce was easy to recreate. However, the person at the winery told me the sauce was made from fresh tomatoes. When I questioned them about that they finally told me they were fresh, this summer! They canned their own tomatoes. So canned San Marzano tomatoes are used here in my recipe.

TUSCAN CRACKERS

1 ½ cups all purpose flour	5 oz olive oil
1 ½ cups semolina flour	5 oz water
½ tsp. baking soda	1 Tbs. fresh rosemary -chopped
¾ tsp. baking powder	¼ cup olive oil
1 tsp. salt	1 tsp. coarse salt

In a bowl stir together the flours, baking soda and powder and 1 tsp of salt. Mix well and form a well in the center. In a small bowl mix together the 5oz each of oil and water. Pour into the center of flour mixture along with the chopped rosemary.

Beat with a fork going around the bowl to incorporate the flour, like making fresh pasta. When a moist dough has been achieved, turn out on the counter and knead for 2 minutes. Allow the dough to rest for 20 minutes. Push dough out onto a 10x15 inch cookie sheet. Prick all over with a fork and cut into 1 ½ inch squares. Bake at 350 for 50 minutes. Remove from oven and immediately brush with the ¼ cup of olive oil and sprinkle on the salt. Return to the oven and bake additional 10 to 15 minutes until crisp.

After removing from oven you may brush with additional olive oil.

TOMATO TOPPING

1-28 oz can San Marzano Italian Tomatoes	1 tsp. red wine vinegar
2 garlic cloves-minced	½ tsp. salt
2 tsp. fresh oregano-minced	¼ tsp. pepper
½ tsp. red pepper flakes	2 Tbs. extra virgin olive oil

Drain the can of tomatoes and use the juice for another recipe.
Deseed the tomatoes and discard the juice and seeds and cut the meat into ¼ inch dice.
In a bowl combine the tomatoes with the garlic, oregano, vinegar and salt and pepper.
Stir to combine. Stir in the olive oil and serve with the crisp crackers.

When I have large groups in Tuscany I pull out this recipe to use during the week. Having the maximum of 8 people, you need more recipes to keep everyone busy during class time. We make this early in the week so that there are leftovers to enjoy. I also use it as a topping on grilled chicken breasts during the summer months.

CAPANATA BRUSCHETTA

4 Tbs. olive oil
1 med. eggplant-1/2 inch cubes (3 cups)
1/3 cup onion-chopped
¾ cup celery-chopped
1 red pepper-diced
1 Tbs. garlic-minced
2 Tbs. tomato paste (mixed with ½ cup water)
1/3 cup green olives-pitted & chopped
½ Tbs. capers-drained & chopped
3 Tbs. red wine vinegar
1 Tbs. sugar
2 Tbs. golden raisins
2 Tbs. pine nuts-toasted
2 Tbs. parsley-minced
salt and pepper
bread-sliced thick & toasted

In a colander place the cubed eggplant and salt, allowing it to sit for 15 minutes, then rinse quickly. In a heavy skillet, add 2 Tbs. olive oil and heat.
Add the eggplant and cook 5 minutes. Transfer to a bowl.
In the same skillet, add the other 2 Tbs. olive oil and heat.
Add the onion, celery, red pepper and garlic and cook 5 minutes.
Add the tomato paste mixture, olives, capers, salt and pepper and cook for 2 minutes. Add the vinegar, sugar, raisins and pine nuts and cook 5 minutes, until celery is tender. Add the eggplant back to the skillet with the parsley and cook an additional 5 minutes. Serve with thick slices of Italian bread which have been toasted.

*Year ago I was working on a cookbook titled **Tuscan Wine Country Cooking**. I solicited wineries in Tuscany who had restaurants on their property. I spent two months working with chefs in about a dozen wineries acquiring menus and recipes to publish a cookbook for all to sell in their establishments. That book still sits in a box on the floor of my office and someday will come to fruition. This recipe is similar to one from a chef I worked with during this cookbook adventure of mine. It's called Arancini, or little oranges, because of their shape. It's usually served in restaurants as a way to use up yesterday's risotto. Filling for these rice balls ranges from small pieces of cheese to whole almonds and small meatballs or a bit of meat sauce as a surprise when eating them. You can serve them plain but with my French training background I like to serve them with a simple tomato sauce.*

FRIED RICE BALLS WITH TOMATO SAUCE

Rice Balls	Tomato Sauce
2 cups cooked arborio rice	1 small onion-diced
2 eggs-lightly beaten	1 tsp. garlic-minced
¼ cup parsley-minced	3 Tbs. tomato paste
2/3 cup Parmesan cheese-finely grated	1-28 oz. can whole tomatoes
4 oz. mozz. cheese-cut into ½ cubes	1 cup tomato puree
1 ½ cup dried bread crumbs	2 Tbs. fresh basil-minced
salt and pepper	1 Tbs. fresh oregano-minced
oil for frying	1 bunch scallions-sliced paper thin

For the rice balls; mix together the first 4 ingredients together in a bowl.

Then form into walnut size balls. Make an indentation in the ball and insert the cubed mozzarella cheese. Enclose the cheese. Roll each ball into the dried bread crumbs and fry in 370 vegetable oil until golden. Drain and serve with the tomato sauce.

Tomato sauce: in a saucepan heat 2 Tbs. olive oil and sauté the onions for a few minutes then add the garlic and cook for one minute. Add the tomato paste and cook 3 minutes. Add the whole tomatoes, breaking them up with a spoon. Then add the puree and fresh herbs and season with salt and pepper. Finally add the scallions and cook for about 30 minutes.

In the fall, nuts abound from the many trees in the area. Hazelnuts, walnuts and chestnuts drop from the trees to the ground and a feast you could make just from these nut crops. Not to mention the wild fennel that grows along the road, grapes from the neighboring vineyards and figs that grow wild on the roadside as we walk up into the hills to see the fantastic views. I often gather products to take back to the villa to prepare an impromptu dinner for my friends.

WALNUT SAUCE WITH PENNE PASTA

¼ cup olive oil
3 garlic-cloves-crushed
½ cup dried bread crumbs
1 cup walnuts-finely chopped

¾ lb. penne pasta
½ cup italian parsley-minced
½ cup Parmesan cheese-grated
salt and Pepper

Bring a large pot of water to boil with 2 Tbs. Kosher salt.

In a large skillet heat the oil till very hot and add the crushed garlic and cook until golden brown 2 to 3 minutes, discard the garlic. To the flavored oil add half of the breadcrumbs, all the walnuts and red pepper flakes and cook until lightly toasted about 3 to 4 minutes.

Remove from the heat and set aside.

In a pot of boiling salted water add the pasta and cook until al dente about 9 minutes.

Just before draining the pasta add 1/3 cup of the pasta water to the walnut mixture.

Drain the pasta and add the pasta into the pan with the walnut sauce. Mix with tongs to combine. Add the parsley and the Parmesan cheese and pour into a platter or bowl and top with the remaining bread crumbs. Serve immediately.

In the United States, we are one of the few countries that eat eggs for breakfast. Egg dishes are usually eaten as a lunch entrée in other countries. When you consume a prepared egg dish you body stays satisfied for long hours after your meal. So in Italy Frittatas originated as a lunch staple for farmers who worked hard in the field long hours after colazione, lunch. I prepared several varieties, so here is one of my favorites. I never use fresh artichoke hearts. Too much work!

ARTICHOKE AND LEEK FRITTATA

2 Tbs. butter
1 leek-washed and sliced thin
9 eggs
1 tsp. fresh rosemary-chopped
1 tsp. salt and ½ tsp pepper

2 Tbs. olive oil
1 can whole artichoke hearts-quartered
¼ cup mozz. cheese-grated
4 Tbs. Parmesan cheese
2 Tbs. balsamic vinegar

In a small skillet melt the butter and sauté the leeks for about 3 minutes. Season with salt and pepper and add the rosemary, remove from the heat. In a bowl beat the eggs.
In a large non-stick skillet add the olive oil and heat.
Add the eggs to the skillet and cook over med. heat and stir lightly.
When the bottom is somewhat set, stir in the leeks, artichoke hearts and the mozzarella. cheese. Continue to scramble until almost set.
Sprinkle on the Parmesan cheese and balsamic vinegar. Place pan in a 400 oven for about 5-10 minutes to finish cooking.
Turn out onto a cutting board and cut into wedges.
Serve immediately with additional balsamic vinegar.

I must admit I eat a lot of chicken and pork for I eat at home a lot more then I eat out. So chicken is easy to prepare, healthful and a great leftover. And chicken is so versatile. Here is one recipe that I like in the fall when celery root is available at the markets. I tried to use this recipe in Tuscany one fall only to find out I was too early for celery root. However, I saw many trucks on the highways laden with this produce never to be seen in Tuscany!

CHICKEN STEW WITH POLENTA, CELERY ROOT & SAGE

5 cups water
1 cup polenta
½ cup flour
salt and pepper
1-4 lb chicken-cut into 8 pieces
6 Tbs. olive oil

1 lg. onion-½ inch dice
1 lg. celery root-peeled cut ¼" dice
2 cups red wine
1 cup tomato sauce
8 fresh sage leaves-chiffonade
1 Tbs. ea parsley and lemon zest-minced

In a large saucepan, bring the water to a boil and add the polenta in a steady stream, whisking constantly. Cook until the polenta is thick as molten lava. Season with salt and pepper. Pour the cooked polenta into a 9x9 pan, smooth the top and allow to cool.

In a shallow pan add the flour and season with salt and pepper. Dredge the chicken pieces in the flour.

In a large dutch oven add the oil and heat and brown the chicken pieces in two batches, then transfer to a platter.

To the dutch oven add the onions and celery root and cook until golden about 10-12 minutes.

Add the wine, tomato sauce, and sage to the pot along with the browned chicken pieces.

Bring to a boil then lower the heat to a simmer and cook about 20-30 minutes.

Cut the cooled polenta into ½ inch squares. Place the polenta on a serving platter or individual plates. Top the polenta with the stew and garnish with the minced parsley and lemon zest. Serve.

Although Tuscany is land locked with the only location in town to buy fresh seafood is from the truck vendor that sits in the square on Thursday mornings in Greve. During the Christmas Holidays, seafood is a very popular staple. Enjoy my seafood stew. It's great the next day as a second serve.

WHITE FISH STEW

1 lb. white fish-cubed	2 celery stalks-sliced ¼ inch thick
4 oz. green olives-pitted	1 med. carrot-sliced ¼ inch thick
1 oz. dried porcini mushrooms	1 med. onion-minced
4 oz. bread-crust removed and cubed	1 garlic clove-minced
2 Tbs. red wine vinegar	8 oz. tomatoes-concasse
2 Tbs. olive oil	3 Tbs. parsley-minced
2 Tbs. butter	tuscan extra virgin olive oil

Chop half of the green olives and leave the other half pitted.

Place the dried mushrooms in a small bowl and top with hot water and allow to sit for 20 minutes to re-hydrate then drain.

Place the cubed bread in a bowl and sprinkle it with the red wine vinegar.

In a dutch oven heat the olive oil and butter and sauté the celery, carrots, and onions until the onions are transparent. Then add the fish, mushrooms, all green olives, soaked bread, tomatoes and parsley, season with salt and pepper and to cook on a low flame for about 20 to 30 minutes until the fish is cooked. Serve in bowls drizzled with olive oil.

When I am not eating chicken I usually eat pork and have many recipes for both. When in Tuscany we drink lots of Chianti. Therefore a recipe is needed using both ingredients.

CHIANTI BRAISED PORK LOIN WITH RED PEPPERS

2 tsp. salt
1 fresh bay leaf, crumbled
pinch of ground allspice
1/2 tsp. ground pepper
1 garlic clove, minced
3 Tbs. olive oil
2 lg. onions- medium diced
2 red bell peppers-cut julienne and halved

4 garlic cloves, chopped
1 bottle chianti wine
1 cup beef broth
1 Tbs. fresh rosemary-minced
1-28 oz. can san marzano whole tomatoes
2 bay leaves
1-4lb. pork loin-rolled & tied

Combine the first 5 ingredients in small bowl.

Pat pork dry and rub with the salt mixture. Cover and chill for 6 to 24 hours.

Preheat oven to 350F. Heat 2 Tbs. oil in heavy Dutch oven or casserole over high heat. Add pork and brown on all sides, about 10 minutes total cooking time. Transfer to plate. Reduce heat to medium and add the remaining 1 Tbs. olive oil to a Dutch oven.

Add the onions and saute until very tender, about 10 minutes.

Add garlic and peppers and saute until peppers begin to soften, about 5 minutes.

Add the wine, beef broth, rosemary, tomatoes, and bay leaves. Add pork, fat side up, and any drippings from the plate. Bring to boil, reduce to a nice simmer, cover and cook until tender about 45 minutes to an hour and a quarter, this depends on your simmer.

When tender and the internal temp is 165, transfer the pork to a platter and let stand 10 minutes before slicing. It should be very tender.

If necessary, boil sauce until reduced to about 4 cups. Season with salt and pepper.

Slice pork and serve with the red pepper Chianti sauce.

For years I have invited guests to the villa when I have students for dinner so that my students get a bit of local color. It seems very enjoyable for everyone. One of our tour guides really liked this recipe as well as the biscotti she was served for dessert. So we packed up the leftovers for her to enjoy at a later time.

LEMON, GARLIC AND ONION CHICKEN

3 cups onions-sliced	1 1/2 Tbs. garlic-minced
2 cups chicken stock	9 fresh thyme sprigs-chopped
2 whole chickens-cut in half	1 Tbs. olive oil
4 lemons-2 sliced very thin and 2 juiced	1/2 tsp. salt and 1/4 tsp. pepper

Place the sliced onions in the bottom of a large baking dish and top with the chicken stock. Under the skin of each half chicken, place lemon slices, minced garlic, chopped thyme and season with salt and pepper.

Place the chicken halves on top of the sliced onions in the baking dish.

Rub the chickens with olive oil and season with salt and pepper.

Top with the lemon juice, making sure you get lemon juice under the skin as well as on top each chicken half.

Place in a 400F oven and bake for about 45 minutes to an hour, basting once during cooking. Cut the chicken into pieces or remove the meat from the bones to serve.

I place the onions on the bottom of a serving platter and top with the chicken pieces.

In the fall, when fennel is in season I pull it from the ground on my walks during the weekend. The bulbs are very small but rich in flavor. To concentrate on the flavor of the fennel I make this very easy recipe and it is usually well received. Of course you can purchase it from most markets. In the States it is usually available all year.

OVEN BRAISED FENNEL

3 fennel bulbs	2 Tbs. fresh lemon juice
¼ cup olive oil	salt and pepper
¼ cup chicken stock	¼ cup Parmesan-Reggiano-grated

Trim the stalks from the fennel bulbs. Chop the fine leaves to measure 2 Tbs.

Split fennel lengthwise in half and cut out the center core. Cut each half into wedges all of about the same size. Place the fennel wedges in a shallow baking pan.

Drizzle with the olive oil, chicken stock and lemon juice. Season with salt and pepper then top with the grated Parmesan Cheese.

Cover with foil and bake in a 400 oven for about 40 minutes and then check for doneness. Continue to bake about 1 hour total. To serve, sprinkle with the chopped fine leaves.

Students tell me all the time they don't have the extra time it takes to use dried beans and they ask if they can use canned beans instead. I act as if they are not talking to me. Using canned beans to me is disgusting. Just think of all that liquid in contact with those beans and for how long. It doesn't take much longer to use dried beans if you manage your time well. When I top the beans with oil just before serving, I use my best Tuscan Olive Oil, which is full of flavor and has an herbaceous peppery taste.

CANNELLINI BEANS WITH FRESH TOMATOES

2 cups dry Cannellini beans	1.5 tsp. salt and 1/2 tsp. pepper
or Great Northern	1 Tbs. + 2-3 Tbs. olive oil
4 garlic cloves-3 peeled & 1 minced	1 tsp. oregano-dried
2 med. celery stalks-cut into 3" pieces	2 cups tomatoes-concasse
1 med. onion-chopped	

In a stock pot, add the beans and cover with water to cover by 2 inches. Bring to a boil for about 2 minutes. Remove from the heat and cover with a lid and allow to soak for 1 hour.

Drain of all the liquid from the beans, rinse them, and add fresh water to cover again by 2 inches. To the pot add the 3 peeled garlic cloves, celery and onion.

Cook for about 1 hour until slightly soft. During the last 15 minutes of cooking, add the salt and pepper. Drain and remove the celery pieces.

Heat 1 Tbs. oil in a skillet and add the minced garlic clove and sauté for 1 minute.

Add the beans with the oregano and season with salt and pepper. Add the tomatoes and cook about 7 minutes. Place the cooked beans on a serving platter; drizzle on the extra 2-3 Tbs. of olive oil to taste.

This is a recipe for a Christmas Dinner menu because of the amount of work involved to produce this recipe. I like this dish because it is different, not your ordinary concoction. The Italians say they invented the crepe. Don't tell the French. We'll just keep it to ourselves, okay?

TIMBALLO OF CREPES

Crepes	Filling
6 eggs	8 oz. pork-cooked and chopped
½ cup flour	8 oz. fresh spinach-chopped & sauteed
pinch of salt	5 oz. mozzarella cheese-grated
2 cup milk	5 med. artichoke hearts-chopped
2/3 cup melted butter	4 oz. Parmesan-grated s & p

Crepes-add the eggs to a mixing bowl and beat lightly.
In another bowl beat together the flour and the milk with the salt.
Beat this dry mixture into the egg mixture. Add 6 Tbs. of the melted butter and mix well. In a 8 inch crepe pan brush with the melted butter to season the pan.
Using a 1/3 cup measure, pour the batter into the pan and cook several minutes.
Turn crepe over and cook for one minute. Repeat process with remaining batter to complete 16 crepes.
To assemble the timballo: Butter a pie tin or sheet pan and place three crepes stacked on top of each other, in the bottom of the pie tin.
Sprinkle on an even layer of ½ of the chopped pork, top with a crepe and layer with ½ of the chopped sauteed spinach.
Top with another crepe and spread on ½ of the chopped artichokes. Place two crepes on top of this last layer and top with ¼ of the grated mozzarella.
Cover with a crepe and sprinkle on ½ of the Parmesan cheese.
Repeat with remaining ingredients for another timballo and bake at 350 for about 20 minutes. Allow to rest for 10 minutes, gently cut into wedges to serve.

This recipe comes from the south of Italy where sweet and sour dishes are usual fare. When you find a recipe for sweet and sour it usually contains pine nuts and raisins, two of my favorite ingredients in cooking and I really like them paired together.

SWEET AND SOUR PEPPERS AND ONIONS

2 Tbs. sugar
1 cup red wine vinegar
1 cup chicken stock
2 Tbs. olive oil
1 red peppers-julienne
1 green peppers-julienne
1 lb. whole sm. onions-peeled
salt and pepper

1/2 cup pine nuts-toasted
1/2 cup raisins

In a saucepan, add the sugar, red wine vinegar and stock and bring to a boil. Add the onions and cook 25 minutes or until tender.

In a skillet heat the olive oil and saute the peppers for several minutes until they just collapse, add the peppers to a bowl. Once the onions are cooked remove from the heat and add the entire contents to the peppers. Add the pine nuts and raisins.

Chill about one hour or until service. Pour into serving bowl, drained or with the liquid.

I love grits not because I live in the south, maybe because I discovered them while attending the C.I.A. I am from Florida and my mother never cooked grits for us as kids. She was from Iowa and she never had them as a child. Polenta is from corn and is very similar to grits. So you doctor them up a bit and serve them as polenta and everyone enjoys the dish. But call them grits and some people won't eat them.

GARLICKY CHEESE POLENTA

2 cups polenta or coarse yellow corn meal
8 cups water
2 tsp. salt

8 Tbs. butter
4 garlic cloves-minced
8 oz Fontina or Mozz Cheese
grated

In a saucepan add the water and salt and bring to a boil. Slowly whisk in the polenta and whisk for at least 5 minutes. After this point you can stir with a wooden spoon and not worry about forming lumps. Cook stirring often for about 25 minutes. Meanwhile melt the butter in a skillet, then add the garlic and cook for 2 minutes.

When the polenta is cooked, fold in the garlic butter and then half of the cheese, pour into a serving dish and top with the remaining cheese to serve.

If polenta cools off, place it in a hot oven for several minutes to reheat before serving.

On Friday we usually prepare a simple brunch menu and always make a cookie. Cookies are easy to prepare, if there are leftovers, I encourage my students to take the cookies with them as they may need a snack in their travels after I drop them at the train station in Florence.

AMARETTI COOKIES

¾ lb. almonds-coarsely ground
2 ½ cups coconut-shredded
¾ + ½ cup sugar

2 tsp. cinnamon
5 egg whites
1 ½ Tbs. amaretto liqueur

In a bowl stir together the ground almonds, coconut and amaretto and set aside. In another bowl combine 3/4 cup of the sugar and the cinnamon and set aside. In a large mixing bowl add the egg whites and beat until foamy. Add the ½ cup of the sugar gradually and continue to beat until the whites form stiff peaks. Fold in the coconut mixture. Spoon the batter onto a cookie sheet lined with parchment paper into walnut sized balls. Sprinkle on the cinnamon sugar mixture and bake at 375 for about 12 minutes or until set. Allow to cool on the sheet pan and then remove them from the parchment paper to serve.

Figs trees are found growing wild along the roadside in Tuscany. At my previous villa that I rented, there were about 4 or 5 fig trees on the property. Figs were abundant. I picked them each morning for breakfast. Then to use up the vast supply, I am always trying new recipes for this wonderful fruit. Here in the south we have figs aplenty. I complained that I could not find a fig tree. So on my birthday, years ago, a couple of friends got together and bought me a fig tree. It is still in its infancy but one day I am hoping for gallons of figs for my own fig preserves. Here is a wonderful recipe that I use when I make my yearly batch of fig preserves and have many to use in other recipes. Plus I eat my fill when picking them and serve with other summer fruits as well.

FRESH FIGS POACHED IN PORT REDUCTION

1 cup water	2 tsp. vanilla
½ cup sugar	2 tsp. corn starch
½ bottle port	1 Tbs. cold water
1 cinnamon stick	16-20 fresh figs

In a medium saucepan combine the water and sugar and stir to dissolve.

Add the port, cinnamon stick, vanilla and bring to a simmer and cook for 15 minutes. Add figs and cook 15 minutes covered. Remove the figs with a slotted spoon to a bowl. Bring the poaching mixture to a boil and cook for 15 minutes.

In a sm. bowl combine the cornstarch with the water.

Add cornstarch mixture to the sauce and boil about 2-3 minutes.

Pour the sauce over figs and chill.

Serve the figs over ice cream and pass the reduction sauce on the side.

Everyone's favorite Italian cookie recipe. We make them during the week but with almonds. They are the best. I usually keep some in the freezer at all times for gifts or when guests arrive so I can serve a simple dessert.

HAZELNUT LEMON BISCOTTI

2 cups + all purpose flour
1 ½ tsp. baking powder
pinch of salt
1/3 cup unsalted butter (2.7 oz.)
1 cup sugar

zest of 1 lemon and minced
¾ tsp. almond extract
3 large eggs
1 cup hazelnuts-toasted & chopped

Line a baking sheet with parchment paper.
In a bowl, combine the flour, baking powder, salt and set aside.
In the bowl of a mixer combine the butter, sugar, zest and almond extract and beat until light and fluffy. Add the eggs, one at a time and beat well after each addition.
Add the dry mixture to the egg mixture and mix well. Fold in the hazelnuts and mix well.
Form a log with the dough in the center of a baking sheet pan, about one inch high and three inches across. Bake at 350F for 25 minutes.
Remove from the oven and allow to cool for about 10 minutes.
Place the log on a cutting board, using a serrated knife slice the log on the diagonal in 1/2 inch pieces and lay cut side down on the cookie sheet and bake for 10 minutes.
Turn the biscuits over and bake an additional 10 minutes. They should be very firm and crunchy, or they will may need more baking time.
Allow to cool before serving, as they cool they will become crisp.

This is a Christmas Cookie that I really like a lot. I do make them but it's easier to buy them at the local coop grocery store in town. You can find them in some restaurants all year long. It's such a treat for me when I see them on a menu for that is what I order. Cookies are very personal among people. I like mine crispy and crunchy and these are.

BRUTTI e BUONI

6 oz + 3 oz almonds
6 oz + 3 oz hazelnuts   pinch cinnamon
4 oz + 4 oz sugar   pinch salt
6 extra large egg whites   ½ tsp. vanilla

Preheat oven to 250.

In the bowl of a food processor add 6oz of each nut with 4 Tbs. of the sugar and process until fine.

Add these nuts to a bowl and set aside.

In the same food processor bowl add the remaining 6oz. of nuts and grind them coarsely. Add them to the bowl of nuts and mix well.

In a mixing bowl add the whites and beat until soft peaks form then add the remaining 4oz of sugar gradually and beat until stiff but not dry.

Then add the cinnamon, salt and vanilla. Fold in the nut mixture gradually.

Add this entire mixture to a large saucepan and cook to dry out the mixture for about 2-3 minutes. Stir with a plastic heat resistant spatula. Scraping the bottom of the pan

On a parchment cover sheet pan drop the cookie batter by heaping tablespoons to form mounds. Bake for 30 minutes and then raise the oven temp to 300 and continue to bake until they are light brown and dried out about 20 minutes more.

As they cool they crisp. Store in an airtight container.

About The Author And Culinary Vacations

Chef John Wils...
Culinary Vacati...

John Wilson is a certified chef and a graduate of the prestigious Culinary Institute of America in Hyde Park, New York.

After working for more than two decades in the restaurant industry, Chef Wilson started Culinary Vacations, Inc. a cooking school vacation in Europe, which has grown to five locations: Normandy and Provence, France, Tuscany and Venice/Maser, Italy and Barcelona/Manresa, Spain. Other locations may be added.

Plus, Culinary Vacations offers "Weekend Gourmet Getaways" in beautiful Asheville, North Carolina as well as Dubois/Jackson Hole, Wyoming, two truly lovely spots in this world to *Get Away*!

Chef Wilson has combined his love of food, wine and travel with his knowledge as a certified professional to bring his expertise to the table in Europe. With more than 22 years of teaching experience, it's a pleasure to learn from this well-traveled and seasoned chef. He has appeared on ABC, CBS and CNN as a guest chef. He also writes for local newspapers and periodicals and is currently working on two more books, *A Tuscany Wine Country Cookbook* and the second in his Tales Series about his years in Provence, France with, hopefully, more to follow.

Chef Wilson is available for private group dinner party cooking classes in Roswell, Georgia and beyond; as well as custom groups of a minimum of four in either of his locations in Europe, when time permits.

Gourmands have a new opportunity to indulge their senses with the combined pleasures of fine food, wine and travel thanks to Chef John Wilson's Culinary Vacations in France, Italy and Spain, established in the fall of 1997.

Five-day cooking classes appeal to "foodies" of all skill levels and offer daily excursions to local food purveyors and points of interest, followed by hands-on instruction and preparation of the main meal of the day.

Each house features beautiful bedrooms and modernized bathrooms; however, its rustic flavor remains complete with hardwood floors, antique furnishings and lovely surroundings. Classroom instruction is held in a large kitchen, accommodating groups of up to 8 students. In addition to daily instruction on regional cuisine and students' hands-on preparation of the meals, the course offers excursions to food purveyors such as olive oil factory, wineries, a local cheese production and a day at the outdoor market, depending on location.

It's so much more unique than a typical vacation. People who love food and have even a slight aptitude for cooking find this type of vacation both relaxing and educational.

Students agree. Mary Ann from New York City says: "It was the most wonderful vacation of my life, and let me tell you, I have been on some great trips".

Classes are only offered twice a year, fall and spring, in each location.

**For more information or to request a brochure,
call toll free 888-636-2073.
In Georgia, call 770-998-2073.
Visit our web-site for additional information at
www.culinaryvacationsinc.com
chefjohnwilson@hotmail.com**

About The Illustrator

Albarosa Redolfi was born in Trieste (Italy) where she studied and run her studio for more than 20 years.

After personal exibitions she decided to work only on custom orders. She is very eclectic and loves to use different media like oil, watercolors and acrylics. The subjects vary from portraits, landscapes to still lifes. She also designs jewels and hand paints original designs on shawls and scarves.

You can find her artwork around the world in Italy, Germany, England, the US and Taiwan.

In the mid 1990's, she decided to move to New York where she lived for several years. After a lot of traveling she decided to move to Tuscany. She lives now in the heart of Chianti region, in the hills around Florence.

Acknowledgements

I would like to first thank Brooks Clark, who suggested I write this book about my students and their misadventures in Tuscany.

To Terry Keller who allowed me to use his cochere, pool house, in Provence for the better part of a month, so that I could take my time putting words to my laptop in the first draft of the book.

To Robert Rodi for his inspiring words.

To all my friends who encouraged me to keep it going and get it to print.

To my watercolorist friend, Albarosa, who supplied the watercolors for this book as well as teaching the watercolor/cooking classes we offer in Europe. Not to mention her insurmountable help while I am in Tuscany each year.

To Joan Parker for her beautiful layout and cover design for this book.

To my friends of many years as both printers and clients, Jay and Darlene Byars.

Thanks to everyone who has helped me along the way in getting my business up and running. There are too many to list here, you know who you are. I will thank those in Tuscany: Giovannella Stianti and Volpaia Winery, Dievole Winery and Mario Junior, Rampini Ceramics-Andrea, Barbara and Tiziana and all the others. Stefania and Gino at LBG leather factory, Claire at the leather store in Castellina, Filippo and Joann at Restaurant Di Lamole for the many years of wonderful food and great service. And last but not least Saverio and Chiara, my hosts while in Tuscany.